Advance Praise for
The Legendary Horseshoe Tavern

At a time when music venues are under attack by gentrification and development, the Horseshoe remains immortal. I've long wondered what those checkerboard floors would say if they could talk. Now they can.
— Alan Cross, music writer and host of the radio series
The Ongoing History of New Music

David McPherson does an amazing thing with this affectionate and informative book.... As someone who has performed there and attended countless shows over the years, it made me feel like I was a witness to something much bigger and more integral to the history of Toronto's ever-changing music scene.
— Ron Sexsmith

David McPherson's tall cold pour of a story left me smacking my lips, nodding my head, and feeling just fine. My recommendation: pull up a chair, drain off one chapter, then another, and the next. Before long, you'll feel absolutely giddy about the Horseshoe and its raffishly distinguished history, Toronto, music, this excellent writer, and the whole wide world.
— Charles McNair, author of the Pulitzer Prize–nominated *Land O' Goshen*

… A glorious two-handed plunge into the loam of the most famous rock and roll club in Canada; digging in the weeds to find the bones that find the ghosts who played there, from Hank Williams to Tom Connors to Frankie Venom to Townes Van Zandt and beyond.
— Dave Bidini, author of *Writing Gordon Lightfoot*

… The Horseshoe is Canada's beating heart of rock 'n' roll. David McPherson's book does a brilliant job illustrating just that.
— Grant Lawrence, the Smugglers

David McPherson has captured the soul and the sweat, the joy and the chaos of the hands-down greatest music parlour in Canada.… From Stonewall Jackson to The Last Pogo, the spirit that is the Horseshoe lives in these pages.
— Colin Linden, Blackie and the Rodeo Kings

David McPherson takes us on a wonderful journey that shows the reader why the club is called the Legendary Horseshoe and where those legends came from.
— Bernie Finkelstein, founder of True North Records

This book truly captures the vibe of the best live music venue in Canada: the sweat, the history, and most of all, the sound — and did I mention the sweat? A love song for the musical grande dame of Queen Street.
— Jay Semko, the Northern Pikes

A valuable document of the Legendary Horseshoe Tavern history.… Jack Starr's legacy lives on!
— Josh Finlayson, Skydiggers

On the eve of its 70th birthday, author David McPherson finally tells the fabled club's story.
— Rob Bowman, Grammy Award–winning author and professor

THE LEGENDARY
HORSESHOE
TAVERN

THE LEGENDARY
HORSESHOE
TAVERN
A COMPLETE HISTORY

David McPherson
Foreword by Jim Cuddy

DUNDURN
TORONTO

Printer: Webcom
Cover images: Patrick Cummings (foreground); Edie Steiner (background)

Library and Archives Canada Cataloguing in Publication

McPherson, David, M.A., author
    The legendary Horseshoe Tavern : a complete history / David McPherson ; foreword by Jim Cuddy.

Includes bibliographical references and index.
Issued in print and electronic formats.
ISBN 978-1-4597-3494-4 (softcover).--ISBN 978-1-4597-3495-1 (pdf).--ISBN 978-1-4597-3496-8 (epub)

1. Horseshoe Tavern (Toronto, Ont.). 2. Rock music--Ontario--Toronto--History and criticism. 3. Popular music--Ontario--Toronto--History and criticism. I. Title.

ML3534.6 C2.M172 2017   781.6609713'541   C2017-904151-7
                                               C2017-904152-5

2   3   4   5   21   20   19   18   17

We acknowledge the support of the **Canada Council for the Arts**, which last year invested $153 million to bring the arts to Canadians throughout the country, and the **Ontario Arts Council** for our publishing program. We also acknowledge the financial support of the **Government of Ontario**, through the **Ontario Book Publishing Tax Credit** and the **Ontario Media Development Corporation**, and the **Government of Canada**.

Nous remercions le **Conseil des arts du Canada** de son soutien. L'an dernier, le Conseil a investi 153 millions de dollars pour mettre de l'art dans la vie des Canadiennes et des Canadiens de tout le pays.

Care has been taken to trace the ownership of copyright material used in this book. The author and the publisher welcome any information enabling them to rectify any references or credits in subsequent editions.

— *J. Kirk Howard, President*

The publisher is not responsible for websites or their content unless they are owned by the publisher.

Printed and bound in Canada.

VISIT US AT

 dundurn.com |  @dundurnpress | dundurnpress | dundurnpress

Dundurn
3 Church Street, Suite 500
Toronto, Ontario, Canada
M5E 1M2

Gracias, Corazón

Without music, life would be a mistake.

— Friedrich Nietzsche

Contents

Foreword

TO UNDERSTAND THE SIGNIFICANCE of the Horseshoe Tavern, one needs to delve into the personal archives of so many Torontonians and visitors to the city to hear the stories of "first time ever" or "best concert" or "mind-blowing after-hours event." The stories are legion. They represent some of the best reflections on the history of the city.

First-ever story: We waited for the Horseshoe to open in order to secure a front-row table to see the legendary pseudo-cowboy Jerry Jeff Walker. I believe we got in and grabbed a table shortly after noon — maybe an apocryphal time, but that is how these stories go. We stayed all day until showtime. The stage was low and, at that time, on the west wall. We were well oiled by the time Jerry Jeff took the stage. He was obviously pleased to see a sold-out house and started in with commitment. A number of songs in, with his long arms swinging, he whacked his guitar on the low-hung ceiling. He cursed and thrust his guitar head angrily into the maze of wires and pipes in the ceiling, thereby rendering the guitar unusable. Frankly, it was our real-life Pete Townsend moment. We could not have been more thrilled and hooted our approvals, to which he gave a sheepish grin.

The story of the Horseshoe Tavern is to a certain degree the history of how Toronto grew up. It starts as a refuge for East Coasters who have come to the city for work and are missing the music and dancing of the homes they have left behind. Count Bazil Donovan, Blue Rodeo bass player, as the son of one of those couples. His parents would venture down to the Horseshoe for some country music and dancing, and to rub shoulders with other East Coasters.

As the city grew and the music scene matured, the Horseshoe stayed true to its friendly roots. By the time our band, Blue Rodeo, was looking to get its first gig in the city, the Horseshoe was the mythical master. I can still remember going down the dark steps to present our cassette to X-Ray MacRae, the rockabilly motorcycle-man music programmer. It was a long and nerve-wracking walk, and as friendly as X-Ray was he had a stack of other cassettes on his desk a foot high. It was not going to be automatic, that was for sure.

So we played a few other places before we got the call. But when we did, it was as exciting as anything that has happened since. Some places just have an aura that makes them more special than the rest, and that says it all about the Horseshoe Tavern. We had grown up in the city hearing about shows at the 'Shoe, and had attended a few, but never thought we would have this opportunity.

How many others have felt the same? Countless, I imagine. The book you are about to read tells the tale of so many decades of entertainers, barflies, doormen, soundmen, scoundrels, poets and can't-miss-but-somehow-did musicians.

The Horseshoe we came to know as a band had some historic nights. Each night the room was full of patrons dressed in neo-cowboy gear, continuing the long tradition of dancing to every song. There were solid, colourful characters — Handsome Ned, Keith Demic, Teddy Fury — all outliers in a supportive creative scene. There were quick-draw contests when Ned played and famous actors and musicians coming to check out a band, and one famous night after the regular closing, the guitarist from Dire Straits, Jack Sonni, whom we knew from New York, where he worked in a guitar store, asked if we could set up a jam. That jam drew all the musicians in town and lasted till six in the morning. Once again, the friendly confines of the 'Shoe had added another entry to Toronto's logbook.

There are not a lot of cities in the world that can boast a stage that has nurtured so many international and local musicians. It has continued virtually without interruption. That alone is an accomplishment. It hearkens back to more innocent "let's just dance and have fun" times. It ties together modern "anything goes" times with those days when Sunday drinking was considered a sin. And all through the painful growing up times, the stage was full of glorious music. Some aspirations withered on the vine, but many flourished. I can say for myself that I was never as happy as I was playing at the 'Shoe when the whole experience was new and unexpected. Again, how many others have felt they found a home away from home at the 'Shoe? Countless, I imagine.

Jim Cuddy
April 2017

Introduction

SINCE 1947, EXCEPT FOR A FEW BLIPS and lean years best forgotten, the Horseshoe Tavern has stood guard just around the corner from Queen and Spadina. While other North American landmarks such as New York's CBGB and the Bottom Line now exist only as commemorative plaques and music memories in people's minds, the Horseshoe has somehow survived for more than seventy years. The more the landscape changes around 370 Queen Street West, the more the tavern remains the same. From the sidewalk, the facade is nondescript; it's no architectural marvel. Inside, the dirty old lady is cramped, cozy and rough around the edges. For music lovers, though, the building, more affectionately known as the 'Shoe, is a shrine. It's a place of firsts: One of the first places in Toronto where you could order liquor. One of the first places you could hear live music. And, one of the first bars to have a TV set. For the long-time staff members who have called the bar home — some for almost three decades — the timeless tavern means family. For many, bonds that became marriages — musical and otherwise — were first formed here. Their memories, along with the list of bands that have played the 'Shoe, are what make the venue so legendary. While some may call it a dive, it's a beautiful dive.

Take a journey with me now. Dive into this icon's past. Begin with a stroll through the 'Shoe's front bar. Stop to peruse the posters, framed autographed photographs, newspaper clippings, and scrawled set lists that line the walls across from the pool table, where most nights you'll find the regulars, who show little interest in the live music coming from the back bar as they shoot a game of stripes and solids. These artifacts tell only some of the stories from the past twenty-five years. Unfortunately, much of the memorabilia from the first half-century of the tavern's existence were either lost or destroyed during the early 1980s. Only a few fragments from those early days remain, such as the huge movie poster advertising the 1963 musical comedy *Bye Bye Birdie*, plastered to the ceiling and peeling away but, like the venue itself, still hanging on near the stage in the back bar. Fortunately, thanks to newspaper reports and memories of those still around to recount their time spent there, there was much research to draw upon for this labour-of-love project.

The Horseshoe is a beacon for music lovers, a pilgrimage destination for those who understand its significance as part of Toronto's rich musical history. One word sums up why it has survived: *passion*. Almost all the owners shared this passion — for the music and for the patrons. As original owner Jack Starr once told *Toronto Star* writer John Goddard, "It was family. I don't mean we had kids there. I mean everyone seemed to know everyone." More important, from the moment Starr booked music in his home away from home in the downtown core, he cared for — and showed congeniality toward — the musicians he booked. They, too, were like family. There are stories of Starr packing picnic lunches for Loretta Lynn and her band to take as they boarded their tour bus. Another famed story you can read about in more detail later in this book is about how Starr's offer to give Stompin' Tom Connors a raise made the late, great Canadian country outlaw cry.

Over the years, thanks to the 'Shoe and its owners, hundreds of Canadian bands have had their starts or have been helped to take that needed step to the next level in their careers. The list is endless: from Dick Nolan and other rising Canadian country stars in the 1960s to Stompin' Tom Connors in the 1970s, to Blue Rodeo in the 1980s, to Nickelback, Rheostatics, Skydiggers, the Lowest of the Low, and the Watchmen in the 1990s. As most Canadian musicians attest, you'd "arrived" if you played the Horseshoe Tavern. Starr began this bequest to the Canadian music industry in the 1950s; today, current majority owner and music aficionado Jeff Cohen, along with his partner Craig Laskey, continue this tradition for the next generation of rising Canadian stars.

That same passion is what led me to write this book. For me, music is the elixir of life. A jolt of live music is always the best medicine when I'm feeling low. The thousands of ticket stubs I've saved over the years — and the lack of funds in my bank account — attest to my love of attending concerts. I came to the Horseshoe Tavern later than most. Like all the

The author, front and centre on the famed checkerboard dance floor, letting the music take him away at an NQ Arbuckle concert at the Horseshoe Tavern in November 2016.

musicians I interviewed for this project, I felt its soul, its historical significance, and its pull from the first time I walked through those doors. A spirit lives there. The musicians feel it. So do the regulars. Even first-timers catch a whiff of these ghosts.

I watched my first show, the Old 97's, in this cavernous, low-ceilinged room more than twenty years ago. Immediately I was hooked. Later, I recall seeing a young Serena Ryder summon the ghost of Etta James — who also once graced that storied stage — with an a cappella version of "At Last" that left the room stunned. I once drank Jack Daniel's from the bottle with the Drive-By Truckers in their dressing room, and did tequila shots on the checkerboard dance floor with singer Jesse Malin following his set on a night the place was packed, fuelled by rumours The Boss was going to join the ex–D Generation singer. People often say about the 'Shoe, "If only these walls could talk." Yes, the stories they would tell. Crazy shit happened inside the dimly lit, blue-collar tavern over the years. I share a few of those tales in these pages, but what this story is really about is a place, a Toronto institution seven decades young that has acquired a personality and mythology all its own. It's part of the social fabric and the history of the city. While much of the Queen Street West strip surrounding the 'Shoe has changed and undergone gentrification, transformed from a desolate street surrounded by factories to a yuppie hangout with high-end fashion stores, the Horseshoe and its raison d'être has remained relatively intact.

Even though the Horseshoe Tavern has always been isolated musically and socially from its surroundings, this venue remains a cultural icon in the Canadian music landscape.

This project combines my love of music with my love of history. Through first-person interviews with musicians who have played the venue to extensive secondary source research, I've dug deep to unearth what has led to the bar's longevity and to discover what makes the 'Shoe so legendary. I hope I've succeeded in bottling this passion and distilling it for your enjoyment.

Come with me now, dear reader, on this journey. Find out why this dame has survived when so many others, like the Beverley Tavern, the Ultrasound, the BamBoo, and the Silver Dollar Room, have come and gone.

Here's to another seventy years of the Horseshoe Tavern. I hope one day my grandkids will walk through those fabled doors at 370 Queen Street West as I once did to hear the latest band on the rise, share a moment in time with fellow music lovers, and discover the ghosts and the soul of the place that are forever etched into the tavern's walls.

1

The Outsider

We shape our buildings, and afterwards our buildings shape us.
—Winston Churchill

DURING THE EARLY HALF of the twentieth century, in the aftermath of two world wars and a half-century of persecution and violent riots and massacres in Eastern Europe — pogroms that saw many attacks on Jews in the Russian Empire — many from these ethno-religious communities immigrated to Canada in growing numbers. A large percentage settled in downtown Toronto and the surrounding suburbs. That was the case with the family of Jack Starr, the original owner of the Horseshoe Tavern, an outsider with the vision to start things up and a man who saw the potential in 368–370 Queen Street West.

Starr's father, Louis — simply called "Pa" by his great-grandson Gary Clairman, as well as by all who knew him — was born in Russia; he was a member of the Russian cavalry during the Russo-Japanese War (1904–05). Supposedly, he was also the bugler in the troop. Japan won the year-long battle that forced Russia to abandon its expansionist policy in the Far East. During the short conflict, Pa, fighting at the front, was shot straight through the heart. Somehow he survived. When the war was over, he, along with the rest of his troop, was briefly arrested for desertion because there had been no communication informing their superiors the conflict had ended. His bravery, sense of adventure, and ability to survive are traits the elder Starr passed on to his son Jack, one of seven children. This dogged determination, entrepreneurial spirit, and can-do attitude served Jack well through the years, and he became an astute small business owner.

By the time the second decade of the twentieth century arrived, Starr's grandfather was tired of the politics, strife, and continual persecution in Eastern Europe. Like so many Polish and Russian Jews before him — and after him — he immigrated to Canada with his wife and two children to provide them with a better life. The Starrs settled on a farm in Whitby, Ontario, right where the 401 exit ramp to the Toronto suburb sits today. Jack was born in 1913 on this rural property. For years, the Starrs used the farm as a way station and inn for Jewish kosher peddlers trying to eke out a living. Later, the family moved to downtown Toronto, buying a house at 153 Manning Avenue, near Dundas and Bathurst.

To mark the Sabbath many Jews did not work on Saturdays, making it difficult for some of these immigrants to get factory jobs. Instead, these new Canadians often started their own businesses and hired their friends and family to work for them. During the early to mid-twentieth century, the garment industry exploded in downtown Toronto and other North American cities, like New York. For a period, the clothing industry was one of the biggest employers in the United States, producing 95 percent of the country's garments. A similar trend occurred north of the border. Early on, the industry in Canada employed mainly Italians and Eastern European Jews, who called it the *schmatta* business (Yiddish for "rags").

Starr was one of the early entrepreneurs who found success in this line of work. In his early twenties, the hard-working first-generation Canadian started in the garment manufacturing business, first learning the trade working as a cutter in a women's wear factory. Before he owned a store of his own, he and his brothers owned a manufacturing company called Hollywood Shirt. Located downtown in what was then referred to as "*Schmatta* Alley," the clothing manufacturer made shirts and other clothes and did a large amount of business through the Sears catalogue. Jack later sold his share of the business to two of his siblings and struck out on his own to begin his next venture: Hollywood Skirt.

Postwar Toronto in the late 1940s and early 1950s was considered a bastion of provincial conservatism, but as more immigrants arrived, and more liquor licences were granted, this perception changed. Toronto evolved into a progressive, cosmopolitan centre of commerce and industry. Queen Street West in the fifties was a working-class neighbourhood inhabited mainly by Italians and Jews.

A Toronto garment workshop, circa 1920s, shows Jewish workers operating sewing machines.

Flash back to 1947. Starr — quiet, congenial, and soft-spoken — surprised his family by purchasing the building at 368–370 Queen Street West from Warren Drug Co. Ltd., with a plan to open a restaurant and bar.

Prior to becoming the Horseshoe Tavern we all know and love, this property, at the edge of Toronto's garment district, changed hands constantly. The building first housed a blacksmith in 1861; later, it shared the space with an engineer and a pair of butchers. Over time, machinists, greengrocers, and many other commercial businesses — from clothing and footwear retailers to the aforementioned drugstore — called the address home. Nothing ever really stuck for long until Starr arrived with his vision.

While it's a coincidence that a stable once resided in the space of Starr's tavern, it's appropriate — in the ensuing years the Horseshoe became home to some of the top acts from Nashville and the stomping grounds for future members of the Grand Ole Opry. Since the property also once housed a blacksmith's shop, it's possible that's where Starr came up with the name. Or, perhaps he was not aware of this historical fact and the name came about simply because he sensed the property, like a horseshoe, was lucky. What is known is that Starr was dabbling in real estate at the time, and the purchase surprised his family. Daughter Natalie Clairman, née Starr, recalls having just come home from summer camp when her father shared the news that he was leaving the ladies' wear manufacturing business: "Honestly, I don't know what put that bee in his bonnet. I think he just got tired of doing that and somehow he got it into his head to open a restaurant."

Over the course of months of sweat and hard labour, Starr invested about $150,000 into the business and built the tavern from the ground up. First, he gutted the building, knocking down the clapboard stores that then occupied the site. Then, he put in a kitchen, a bar, and seating for close to one hundred patrons. At the time, the new, loosened provincial liquor licence laws (circa 1947) permitted Starr to convert the commercial property to an "eatery-tavern" and start serving alcohol. Naturally, he started the process to obtain one of the city's first liquor licences. This took time and caused Starr some stress. Dealing with government bureaucracy was no different in Starr's time than it is today. Forms needed to be filled out, criteria met, and papers signed, and then one had to wait for approval from the Liquor Licensing Board of Ontario (LLBO).

Some of the biggest opponents to bars such as Starr's obtaining the right to sell liquor either with or without meals were clergy. Reverend J. Lavell Smith of the Church of All Nations, up the street from the Horseshoe Tavern at 423 Queen Street West, denounced the granting of licences to all restaurants in the vicinity of his church. "There are enough drunks on Queen Street as it is, and there is [no] need for more outlets," he told the liquor board. "We had two drunks barge in to our service the other night."

Did Starr bribe someone with a bag of cash to get the paperwork approved and to expedite the government's stamp of approval? There's no one left alive to confirm whether this rumour is true. No matter, eventually Starr succeeded — securing the second Ontario licence granted by the newly created LLBO, shortly after the Silver Rail on Yonge Street, which opened earlier that year on April 2.

When Starr tried to patent and register the tavern's name, he ran into another stumbling block. As Natalie Clairman recalls, "He initially had a really hard time getting the name 'Horseshoe' patented because of the similarity to Billy Rose's famed Diamond Horseshoe nightclub in New York City … there was some sort of infringement rights; eventually, he got it. Where he got that name from, I honestly don't know, because my dad never went to the races and he wasn't a gambler. Maybe he just thought it would be lucky."

A postcard of the Horseshoe Tavern depicting what it looked like, circa the early 1950s.

Luck certainly played a part in Starr's early success. On December 9, 1947, the Horseshoe Tavern officially opened. In the December 12, 1947, edition of the *Toronto Daily Star*, an ad for the newly opened establishment called it Toronto's "Finest Eating Place" and proclaimed, "It's the Rave of Toronto! You and your friends are cordially invited to the newly opened Horseshoe Tavern, where the delicious food and distinctive atmosphere is second to none…. Sunday dinner served from 2 to 8 p.m."

Starr's idea was to run a tavern for the city's workers and "outsiders," those not part of the social elite — the blue-collar toilers in the garment and textile factories, the cops who kept the streets safe, other downtown denizens and not-so ne'er-do-well characters, wayfarers who roamed the city streets. The tavern's first licence had a legal capacity of eighty-seven seats. In those early days, the bar's focus was on value: good food, cold beer, and liquor. Another first, according to *Time* magazine: the Horseshoe was the first bar in Canada to have a television. This happened in 1949.

Starr expanded the space over the years, buying the property next door and enlarging the Horseshoe until it eventually sat five hundred patrons. Soon, live music would rain from the rafters seven nights a week.

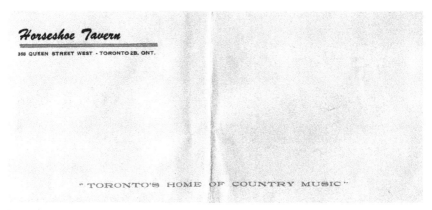

Horseshoe stationery.

* * *

While he stood only about five foot four, Jack Starr had a big heart and knew a few things about running a business. In a famed picture taken years later with one of his favourite Nashville performers, Little Jimmy Dickens, Starr looks like a giant next to the diminutive four foot eleven rhinestone cowboy. Like his personality, the shows Starr booked and promoted were always larger than life. The room had a barn-like vibe then, and even though it's half the size today, it still feels like a rural retreat.

There's no sensible reason why a tavern that hosted country music ended up on this stretch of street. Despite this anomaly, Toronto music lovers around the world are thankful. What did Starr know about running a bar? Not much, but he knew how to run a successful business. And, he was also driven — possessing a work ethic inherited from his father. During the years he ran the bar, he rarely left. He was a fixture at the door; after the doorman, he was usually the next person who greeted you upon entering the building. Before shows and during intermissions, he'd walk from table to table saying hello to the regular patrons, making sure his adopted family always enjoyed themselves.

Starr left a lasting impression on all the artists who played within those four walls, as well as with all the men and women who drank a cold beer on a stool in the front bar or stopped in for a late-afternoon game of pool. Starr was fair. Everyone respected him. Natalie Clairman recalls, "People loved him. He quickly became a fixture on Queen Street. All the policemen knew him, including all the undercover cops. They never paid for a drink in

A view of the cityscape near Queen and Spadina in the mid-1920s near the intersection where Jack Starr would later open the Horseshoe Tavern.

his bar. Every Christmas, he would host a big party at the Horseshoe for the police. All the people from the *schmatta* business also knew him too ... he was very friendly and very outgoing."

Starr was also a regular at neighbourhood restaurants like Lichee Garden, which opened in 1948 and boasted an enormous dining room with a capacity to serve as many as 1,500 customers a day. Provincial and federal political leaders and other celebrities often dined there. Lichee Garden even had a band and offered dining and dancing until closing at 5:00 a.m. Whenever Starr showed up, a murmur of excited chatter would go through the place; everybody knew his name and loved to see him. Clairman remembers a dad she rarely saw during those early days when he was running and expanding the business: "It was a night business. He would go into the club after dinner, stay until it closed, and be there early the next morning to tally up the bar sales from the previous night and do inventory."

An avid and accomplished golfer, Starr took rare breaks from running his beloved tavern in the summers to tee it up at Oakdale Golf and Country Club, near Downsview, where he was a member. A newspaper report from 1954 mentions Starr winning the annual Toronto Hotel Association Championship. Following his round, the businessman sometimes took an afternoon siesta before heading back to the bar. Some of Gary Clairman's earliest memories, as a nine-year-old, are of going down to the bar on a Sunday afternoon, eating a banquet burger with fries, and just hanging out with his grandpa. He recalls:

(Top and bottom) Looking eastward on Queen Street to Spadina Avenue on October 12, 1933, fourteen years before Jack Starr opened the Horseshoe Tavern at 368–370 Queen Street West.

Sometimes, if I slept over at my grandparents' house, Jack would get up and we would go down to the Horseshoe together before it opened. There was a trapdoor behind the bar where he kept the safe. That room is still there. He would open the safe, and it would be full of one-dollar bills because everything from a beer to a shot of liquor cost one dollar in those days. There would be stacks and stacks and stacks of ones. I would help him count them. Then, we would put them in bundles of twenty-five or fifty to take to the bank.

In later years, these family moments at the Horseshoe Tavern continued. As Pa was then in his nineties, living alone in an apartment, Starr would pick up his dad at 8:00 a.m. and take him down to the bar. While Starr tallied up the receipts and took inventory from the previous night's sales, his dad kept busy. Natalie Clairman recalls, "My grandfather would take a shot glass, go around the bar and pour the rye, Scotch, and gin — the dregs of whatever was left in the glasses on all the tables into his glass — then he would sit in a chair, drink it back, and fall asleep for the rest of the morning until Jack took him home!"

Despite the presence of lowly citizens who were regular barflies at the Horseshoe, fights were rare. Mixing with these drifters and law-abiding country and western music lovers were detectives — rough, hard-nosed characters — as well as criminals in the making who turned to the wrong side of the law to survive and make ends meet. These bookies, bootleggers, and bank robbers were the people below the veneer of the city's stereotype of "Toronto the Good." One of the tavern's most famed patrons in those early years was the mastermind bank-robbing bandit Edwin Alonzo Boyd, who later escaped not once — but twice — from Toronto's Don Jail, and other members of his notorious gang drank there as well.

Sergeant of Detectives Edmund "Eddie" Tong's old battered Buick was often seen parked outside one of the many newly opened taverns in downtown Toronto, including the Horseshoe, during those years. As Brian Vallée writes, "People called Tong 'the Chinaman' because of his name and his black hair, which he combed back off his forehead." Tong kept an eye on the underbelly of Toronto, where the likes of Boyd and his gang dwelled. Starting in

1949, the cop routinely visited places like the Silver Rail on Yonge Street, the Holiday Tavern at Queen and Bathurst, and the Horseshoe Tavern at Queen and Spadina. Since opening and being some of the first establishments to obtain liquor licences in the province, these bars had quickly become the watering holes of choice for Toronto's criminals and their hangers-on. Tong and his partner at the time, Jack Gillespie, would go into the bars just to let these patrons know they were around and they were watching.

Barkeep Lennie Jackson was a drifter, a pool shark, and one of these hangers-on; he landed a job at Starr's tavern after moving to Toronto from Niagara Falls. As Vallée writes, "It wasn't long before Lennie Jackson decided he wanted some of the better things in life, and that the way to get them was not by waiting on tables in a bar, but by robbing banks." Jackson ended up quitting the Horseshoe and becoming a wanted man for his role in a series of bank robberies with the Boyd Gang. He was eventually shot by Gillespie, but not before he and his fellow partner in crime, Steve Suchan, shot and fatally wounded Tong in March 1952.

While there are a couple of old newspaper stories about shootings near the Horseshoe in the 1950s, these events were rare. Asked about this by the *Globe and Mail*, long after he had retired and the bar was set to celebrate its fortieth anniversary, Starr, then seventy-seven, replied, "Oh, there were a few freak incidents like that. In the early days, we spent about 90 percent of the time at the door keeping out the type of people we didn't want in. But over the years we had a cross-section of all kinds: college kids, doctors, lawyers, and businessmen."

Besides this eclectic cast of colourful characters, most of Starr's regular patrons were good-time folks from the East Coast. Daughter Natalie Clairman remembers, "At a time when the economics in the Maritimes was not very good, they were migrating to Toronto. They were country music fans, so they eventually persuaded my dad to bring in some music. It sounds simple, but that's as simple as it was." Adds Natalie's son, Starr's grandson Gary Clairman, "I'm sure Jack became a fan of country music, but it's not like he was playing it around the house. He was smart enough to know though that it was going to fill the place."

The country and western acts certainly helped pack the establishment. Beginning in the early 1950s and lasting until he retired in the mid-1970s, Starr's booking policy helped fill the Horseshoe's coffers for twenty-five years.

Marvin Rainwater was the first act Starr hired. Rainwater, an American country and rockabilly singer and songwriter, had several hits during the late 1950s, including "Gonna Find Me a Bluebird" and "Whole Lotta Woman" — a number one record in the United Kingdom. The musician was known for wearing stage outfits based on traditional aboriginal clothing; he was part Cherokee.

The first country performer, though, was Shorty Warren, from Jersey City. As Starr later told the *Globe and Mail*, "Country music was not a socially accepted genre at the time, so the tavern provided an escape for country music lovers."

Starr's business acumen, marketing and promotional powers quickly built the Horseshoe Tavern from an intimate eighty-seven-seat restaurant serving food, beer, and liquor, and catering to a neighbourhood clientele, to a five-hundred-seat music venue serving the growing musical needs of expats and migrant workers from Atlantic Canada — and also satisfying the growing legions of Hogtown's country music fans. Stompin' Tom Connors recalls this reputation in his second memoir: "Everybody who was a country fan and who landed in Toronto for any reason, either by plane, car, bus, or train, for any length of time, sooner or later wound up paying a visit to the Horseshoe."

2
Nashville North

I won't stay home and cry tonight like all the nights before
I've just learned that I don't really need you anymore
I found a little place downtown where guys like me can go
And they've got bright lights and country music

Bright lights and country music, a bottle and a glass
Soon I'll be forgetting that there ever was a past
And when everybody asks me what helped me forget so fast
I'll say, "Bright lights and country music"

— Bill Anderson and Jimmy Gateley,
"Bright Lights and Country Music"

YOU CAN MAKE A CASE THAT the high point of the Horseshoe Tavern's existence was during its heyday as a country music bar. I am not talking about the mainstream country you hear over the airwaves today. I am talking about vintage country, the kind your grandparents tuned in to on their transistor radio after a hard day's work — listening to a station from Wheeling, West Virginia, or Nashville, Tennessee, at the farthest reaches of their FM dial. From the mid-1950s to the late 1960s at the Horseshoe, lineups around the block were common. The tavern's stationery proclaimed, "Toronto's Home of Country Music." Seven nights a week, honky-tonk tunes spilled out onto Queen Street. Nashville legends — and future Country Music Hall of Fame members — picked and strummed their guitars and sang their timeless songs on the 'Shoe's stage to adoring audiences. Some of them even recorded albums at Starr's bar. You could see the admiration all the Nashville acts had for the Toronto venue and for its charismatic owner. Take the famed American bluegrass musician Mac Wiseman, for example. As he writes on the sleeve of his 1965 album *Mac Wiseman Sings at the Toronto Horseshoe Club*, "The Horseshoe uses top country & western artists fifty-two weeks a year and the great success being enjoyed by this fine club must be attributed to Mr. Jack Starr and his friendly, efficient staff. Mr. Starr is not only a very smart club manager; but he's also a wonderful person and a true friend of country music. Anytime you are around Toronto, drop in at the Horseshoe, and tell Jack — Mac sent you."

This is a part of the tavern's rich history few know about. Many of those famous performers from that era have passed on; others have fuzzy memories of those days. Thankfully, a handful of these musicians — and some of the fans — are still around to share their stories. Allow me to transport you back to those good, old country days.

* * *

Donn Reynolds, Canada's "King of the Yodellers," poses outside the Horseshoe Tavern.

Fifty years ago, the Horseshoe was known in the music industry as Nashville North and was a regular stop for the top country stars of the day, including those great acts from the Grand Ole Opry. The list of performers who graced the 'Shoe's stage during this period could fill this book. The following is just a sampling of the country heavyweights who played there: George Hamilton IV, Faron Young, Kitty Wells, Bob Luman, Ferlin Husky, Little Jimmy Dickens, the Carter Family, Willie Nelson, Waylon Jennings, Loretta Lynn, Bill Anderson, Charley Pride, and Tex Ritter.

Nearly every country superstar of the time, save Hank Williams, Porter Wagoner, and Buck Owens, played there. Although according to Wayne Tucker, who wrote the definitive biography of Dick Nolan — the leader of the Horseshoe's house band during this period — Owens, known for pioneering the Bakersfield sound, did make an unannounced, impromptu appearance.

> Buck Owens was a big name in the 1960s and his fees were high. For this reason he didn't actually play the Horseshoe. But one night Buck dropped into the 'Shoe just to hear the music. He was keeping a low profile amongst the crowd and he had asked Dick, the emcee, to keep his presence a secret. Dick knew that Buck had a temper but he ignored his request and announced that he was in the audience. Then to stir the pot he said: "Would you like to hear him sing?" So an angry Owens had no choice but to take the stage and do a number for free.

When the club was full, it was *full*, which was nearly every night. Bill Anderson, Tex Ritter, and Willie Nelson were some of Starr's favourite acts. Years later, many performers still recall with fondness the genteel Jewish businessman who treated them so well: "Every Christmas, there were a load of turkeys in the backroom for the band," recalls Roy Penney, who played lead guitar in the house band in the 1960s. "He and I used to swap cufflinks; that was our annual tradition. He always treated the band well. On Saturday matinees we would get a big steak dinner on the house."

Russell deCarle, founder of Prairie Oyster, shares a story about a time when, years ago, the six-time Juno Award winners were rehearsing for an album in Nashville at SIR Studios and Waylon Jennings was getting ready for a tour and rehearsing in the same space: "We would meet at the water cooler and have a coffee with Waylon every afternoon for about half an hour for four days. One of the first things he asked, when he found out we were from Ontario, was about Jack Starr and the Horseshoe … he had nothing but great memories of working there."

Live music had come to the Horseshoe in a roundabout, unorthodox way. Some of Starr's most loyal customers were blue-collar workers; many were Maritimers who had arrived in Toronto in the fifties and sixties looking for jobs. Similar to Starr's own father's reasons for journeying from Eastern Europe to Ontario, these dreamers sought opportunities and better lives for their families. In an editorial called "Finding the Heart of Canada," published in the *Toronto Star* on May 7, 2002, Bernard Heydorn, author of *Walk Good Guyana Boy* and a past member of the *Star*'s community editorial board, captures the 'Shoe's clientele, whom he mixed with back in the 1960s and early 1970s: "Many of the patrons were folks who came from outside the city. They were migrants from rural Canada, northern Ontario, and down east. There were farmers and fishermen, truck drivers and factory workers, coming together from the heartland of a great nation."

Other patrons were just drifters and society's outsiders, looking for adventure, escape, or a change of scene. Greg Marquis eloquently captures these characters and their stereotypes in his essay "Confederation's Casualties: The 'Maritimer' as a Problem in 1960s Toronto": "In the eyes of urban Ontarians, Maritimers had several characteristics. They were fatalistic young drifters who lived off welfare, drank heavily, engaged in violence, listened to country and western music, and broke the law in order to survive."

Despite Marquis's assessment, the violent stereotype of these East Coast emigrants did not hold true at the Horseshoe Tavern. Violence was rarely an issue. Everyone came for a good time and respected Starr enough to not cause trouble. So, how did the Horseshoe go from being a restaurant that served some of the best prime rib in Hogtown and was a watering hole for blue-collar factory workers, rounders, and cops in the downtown core to becoming Canada's top country and western bar, with lineups on Queen Street that stretched for several blocks on Saturday nights?

The evolution was simple.

Starr always put his customers first. And all the Horseshoe's customers had two things in common: they liked to drink, and they liked to dance.

One afternoon, Jack left his office in the back of the club to check on his customers, as was his habit. As he was walking through the bar, talking to the folks who were there, one of the loyal customers chirped, "Hey, Jack. You should start booking live music here." To which the owner replied, "Okay. What kind of music do you like?" "Country, of course," the customer said.

And so country and western music it was.

The genre was certainly not something Mr. Starr and his family listened to at home on the radio. "Jack knew how to bring the music in, but he wasn't very musical and we all hated country and western music!" recalls his daughter Natalie Clairman, whose family still owns the building. "We never went down there at all."

But, being a shrewd and smart businessman, Mr. Starr knew satisfying his customers was crucial to running a successful small business. As he once told the *Toronto Star*, "I didn't know anything about country music in those days, but I looked around and I figured that, with all the other types of entertainment available in the city, there must be room for a country place."

The Edison Hotel on Gould Street had a foothold on Toronto's nascent country scene; later, the Brunswick House on Bloor and the Matador at Dovercourt and College hired country acts. But the Horseshoe would acquire a reputation for booking the best — Nashville's top talent. (It also became an unwritten rule that if you played the Edison, you didn't play the Horseshoe, and vice versa.)

So Starr got to work, replacing the kitchen with a stage (in the backroom where the bar is located today) and renovating the space — gradually expanding the available space fivefold by purchasing neighbouring stores. By the time Starr started booking live music, the seating capacity had increased from eighty-seven to five hundred. An assortment of square and round tables with chairs were nestled right up to the stage, which was only slightly raised off the black-and-white checkered tile floor that remains to this day. With this new setup, the performers and audience melded into one.

*   *   *

Bazil Donovan, the bassist for Blue Rodeo, grew up in Toronto's west end. His parents were regulars at the Horseshoe — one of the many couples who had migrated from the East Coast. His mom was a Cape Bretoner, and his dad was born in Prince Edward Island but grew up in Halifax. Bazil's dad loved country music, while his mother was more into rock 'n' roll — Elvis Presley and Buddy Holly. "He watched what became The Band [former members of Ronnie Hawkins and the Hawks] at the Concord a lot. My dad went to all of those places. My mom was seventeen when she had me," Donovan recalls. "They arrived in Toronto in April 1956. My dad was twenty. Needless to say, they were out to explore 'the big city,' and the things that mattered to them the most were listening to music and dancing. I remember him bringing me home autographed pictures of some of the people he saw play at the Horseshoe, such as Stonewall Jackson. I didn't know who the guy was, but he said, 'Keep this, and someday it will be worth something.' Of course, I never did."

Juanita Garron arrived in Toronto in the early 1950s. Like many before her, she, too, quickly fell in love with the country music scene Starr started. This passion for country and western led to a job checking coats at the Horseshoe. From this vantage point, Garron heard the music nightly and met many of the Nashville stars of the day. Starr was so impressed by Garron's amiable personality, and her good ear, that he expanded her duties over the years — sending her on the road. Garron took scouting trips to Wheeling,

Stonewall Jackson, one of the most popular country artists of the 1960s, was a regular at the Horseshoe Tavern.

West Virginia, and Tennessee to see these legendary musicians and other rising stars at the Grand Ole Opry and other western venues. According to her obituary (Garron passed away on December 22, 2014), in her lifetime she visited this country music shrine eighty-eight times. "She was approachable, awesome, kind, and thoughtful," recalls Doreen Brown, a country artist and one-time friend of Garron's. "She loved to talk about country music. She didn't drink, smoke, or swear, but she was hilarious!" With a great deal of encouragement from the musicians she met, Garron later started singing country and western Bible songs and hymns. Her talent was recognized by the major country and western associations in Ontario and she was well known for her rendition of "One Day at a Time" and for singing Canada's national anthem at the opening and closing of Ontario's country and western music associations during their meetings, jamborees, and other events. It's no surprise to learn that Starr later presented his former coat check girl with a certificate naming her the "Mother of Country Music."

For more than a decade, tour buses, all with Nashville plates, were a common sight in the vicinity of the Horseshoe Tavern, and they often parked in the back alley. No matter the weather, country music fans lined up hoping to share a few words with their idols and snag an autograph. Usually, the musicians obliged. During intermissions, members of the feature band or the house band would go from table to table selling the headliner's latest LP. If the show was presented by one of the major country record labels of the day — such as RCA — the artist would set up a booth near the coat check to sign LPs and photographs, and to shake hands with the regulars.

Bob Gardiner, a country music photographer and journalist, was a regular at the Horseshoe throughout the 1960s and early 1970s. When his marriage broke down, he lived in a boxcar for a while on the Canadian National Railway property, but each evening he headed up to the tavern on Queen. The octogenarian recalls a particular fond memory of an interview he conducted for Walter Grealis's *RPM* magazine with Grand Ole Opry and Country Music Hall of Fame member Ernest Tubb:

> I went down to the Horseshoe in the early afternoon. It wasn't a great day … it was raining cats and dogs. Ernest let me on to his tour bus that was parked on a side alley in behind the club. We were just getting acquainted before

the interview when Ernest looks out the door and sees all these people standing in the rain. He's dressed in this beautiful Nudie suit and says to me, "Before we get down to business, I have to go out and meet these people. If they are willing to stand out there in the rain, I appreciate that and need to let them know." After chatting with his fans, Ernest came back in and he looked like a drowned rat. His beautiful Nudie suit was soaked. He went to the back of the bus, changed, got spruced up again, and then we had a nice conversation.

Later that night, Tubb opened his show at the 'Shoe to raucous applause, and began by playing his hit "Thanks a Lot."

Every weekend, a similar scenario played out. Couples congregated at this country music shrine to worship their musical idols like Tubb, whose career spanned more than four decades and symbolized the heart and soul of Texas honky-tonk. Women with beehives, stretchy pants, and blouses with puffy sleeves came in with cowboys on their arms; the men sported skinny string ties, V-neck sweaters, and padded jackets. Most had pompadours and long sideburns. The women hummed, clapped, and sang along to their favourite songs; the men hooted, hollered, and banged on the tables for one more encore before closing time at 1:00 a.m. On busy weekends, up to thirty staff members would be hustling trays of beer from the bar to the tables throughout the performances. Mickey Andrews, who was in the house band for four years from the late 1960s to the early 1970s, recalls towers of empty beer cases stacked in the corners of the bar by Sunday night.

Charley Pride was another regular at the country shrine on Queen Street. Bob Gardiner knew him well. The photographer used to show up early for all the concerts, head backstage, and hang out with the various artists. He always had his camera bag with him, and often put it in the corner of the dressing room. "I remember one night being there before a show with Charley," says Gardiner. "After the show, I had to go back to get my bag, and it was gone! I turn and look at Charley sitting in his chair, and he had this big, sheepish grin on his face. I knew he had hid it on me … he was a bit of a joker."

* * *

A feature article in the *Toronto Daily Star* in March 1964 proclaimed, "Make Way for the Country Sound." In it, journalist Morris Duff says, "At a time when many other clubs are pushing panic buttons, those featuring country and western are doing business, even when it rains or snows." The paper had a weekly column, Around the Ranch, with the latest country and western news, and the city even had a magazine dedicated to covering the genre called *The Country Gentleman*.

During this era, radio also helped get the word out about the Opry stars. Bill Bessie hosted a weekly program on Saturdays between noon and 1:00 p.m. on CBC Radio in which he would interview the Nashville stars who were playing the Horseshoe or the Edison that night. CFGM Radio, based in Richmond Hill, Ontario, also helped spread the country and western gospel. Starting in 1968, the FM station broadcast of country hits was fifty thousand watts strong, twenty-four hours a day, seven days a week. It was the first Canadian station to program country music exclusively; later, in

Jack Starr with future Country Music Hall of Famer Loretta Lynn in the late 1960s.

1976, the broadcaster even produced a show dedicated to the genre, called *Opry North*, that mimicked Nashville's Grand Ole Opry. The popular syndicated show continued until CFGM ended its country music policy in 1990.

As country music grew, the station increased its wattage and expanded its listener base. Alan Fisher was a DJ for CFGM in those years, and he had the chance to chat with many of the Nashville stars when they played in Toronto, frequently at the Horseshoe. He would also introduce them in the evenings as the emcee when the radio station sponsored some of the shows.

"One of the features of the show had me interviewing one of the stars who would be appearing in town that week, either at the Horseshoe Tavern or at the Edison on Yonge or from the *Nashville North* CTV show," Fisher recalls in his book *God, Sex and Rock 'n' Roll*. "I got to meet and interview a lot of them, including Bill Anderson, Loretta Lynn, George Hamilton IV, Bob Luman, and many more."

Before Bernie Finkelstein went on to make his mark in the music industry, managing the likes of the Paupers and Bruce Cockburn and founding True North Records, he was just an adolescent with little interest in school and a growing love for anything to do with music. He was also a friend of Fisher's. In later years Blackie and the Rodeo Kings, another band he managed, was a mainstay at the 'Shoe, but he says his first time walking through those timeless doors as an underage teenager remains his fondest.

> I remember going with Al [Fisher] down to the Horseshoe one afternoon when he was a DJ working for CFGM. I had never been in there before, and my first impression was of it being quite glitzy. Ferlin Husky was playing. Anybody who knows anything about country music knows "Wings of a Dove," which was his big record. That remains even today an unforgettable experience. I'll never forget that first time at the Horseshoe. For me, the real excitement was all those country-music-loving women in their bouffants. Who knew what mysteries lurked under those wild hairdos?

Ferlin Husky was one of the stars Fisher interviewed. He played the Horseshoe many times, including that memorable first night for Finkelstein in 1969. "Wings of a Dove," a gospel song, was a number one country hit for him in 1960 and one of his signature songs. The future Country Music Hall of Famer (2010), who went on to sell more than twenty million records, was one of the more popular performers at the venue in the late 1950s and 1960s.

The Horseshoe didn't just draw residents of Hogtown looking for a hoedown. Many came from the outskirts of Toronto; some drove more than a hundred kilometres to hear that good old country music, and some even flew! Jack Starr told Dick Brown, in a feature piece for *The Globe and Mail* in 1973, about a time a mother and her daughter flew up on a Friday evening from St. John's just to catch a performance by Husky, and then jumped on a plane back to Newfoundland on Saturday afternoon.

Country fans could not get enough of the Toronto twang and the dancing that usually accompanied it. After the Horseshoe wound down, shortly after 1:00 a.m., their appetite for more had to be satiated. To keep the party going, Toronto's first after-hours country and western club, the Golden Guitar, opened in 1964, and then Beatrice Martin, the Horseshoe's hostess with the mostest for more than a decade, opened her own after-hours club that same year. Aunt Bea's short-lived Nashville Room on Spadina, south of College, catered to the country music fans' desire to keep the honky-tonkin' going long into the wee hours. According to reporter Jack Batten, Aunt Bea had neatly coifed silver-blond hair. She was always smiling, and her smile was contagious. She made friends with everyone she met. In an interview with the *Toronto Daily Star*, Aunt Bea described how her speakeasy came to be.

> Country fans are such a loyal bunch, you know. They can never get enough of their music. And the musicians are the same — they like to keep on playing all night. On weekends, especially, nobody wants to quit after the Horseshoe closes at 1:00 a.m. and for years they all kept saying to me, "Oh, Aunt Bea" — everybody calls me that — "why don't you start another place for afterwards." Finally, I did, and now the Nashville Room's open until four or five in the morning every Saturday and Sunday. And we all have a wonderful time, listening and dancing and talking.

Gary Clairman, Jack Starr's grandson, pretends to play the drums at Aunt Bea's after-hours club one Sunday morning.

For a brief period during the Horseshoe's heyday as a country music mecca, Bea's Nashville Room, with a capacity of about 250, was packed every weekend night long after last call ended at the 'Shoe. It was so popular that many patrons were turned away at the door.

The Matador, which opened in 1964 and was run by the late Ann Dunn — a single mother of five who, as the story goes, wanted a place that wouldn't interfere with her parenting duties — lasted a lot longer. The after-hours club quickly found a home as a notorious booze can and hip honky-tonk spot that satisfied the appetites of patrons and musicians alike. These twenty-four-hour party people wanted to carry on the celebrations on the weekends into the wee hours, long after the Horseshoe and the other honky-tonk bars had closed. Many of the artists who'd been booked at the Horseshoe, along with a parade of patrons, headed over to this speakeasy at Dovercourt and College once the 'Shoe had closed down — keeping the conversations and the music going until 5:00 a.m. Cowboy boots were nailed onto the wall behind the stage. Here, only real traditional country music was played. There was a house band at the Matador, but everyone who went there was like one big family. Performers swapped songs and shared the stage. In between sets, everyone went upstairs to mingle, or downstairs, where there was always a high-stakes poker game being played. Barnboard walls marked the turn-of-the-century building that was once a ballroom and dance hall for soldiers on leave during the Great War. Naturally, signs with "Cowgirls" and "Cowboys" indicated the route to the washrooms.

Over the years, patrons had the chance to witness legendary early-morning jam sessions by the likes of Johnny Cash, Johnny Paycheck, and Conway Twitty. In the 1970s, the Matador was also the stompin' grounds for Stompin' Tom Connors following his Horseshoe gigs. Later on, Canadian folksinger-songwriters Joni Mitchell and Leonard Cohen found their way there, as did many other celebrities; Cohen even wrote the song "Closing Time" about the after-hours club. The venue continued to operate until 2006.

Back at the Horseshoe, the entrepreneurial Starr was looking for ways to expand his business. In the early part of the 1970s, with Martin as the hostess, on long weekends throughout the summer bus tours left from the Horseshoe's door and travelled the white line south to Music City, visiting the sites like the Country Music Hall of Fame and taking in performances at the Grand Ole Opry. Three hundred music lovers would line up for a chance to get a seat on one of seven buses that made these regular pilgrimages to the home of country music. Sometimes, Starr would tag along on these road trips.

Baseball fence at the old Maple Leaf Stadium at Bathurst and Lake Shore, with a banner advertisement for the Horseshoe Tavern from the early 1950s.

During this period, Starr expanded his business to include music publishing. He promoted big packaged shows outside the Horseshoe at places like Maple Leaf Stadium, the old baseball stadium on Lake Shore Boulevard, just south of where the Tip Top Tailors lofts stand today. Starr managed the artists and manufactured and sold their LPs and other merchandise at their shows, since the Nashville acts had a hard time bringing products across the border in those days.

* * *

Bill Anderson, a Nashville songwriter who is still playing and recording today at the age of seventy-nine, keeps a special place in his heart for the Horseshoe Tavern. During the 1960s, Whisperin' Bill — as he was affectionately known for his soft vocal style — was a regular, playing the Horseshoe at least once or twice a year. A Grand Ole Opry member since 1961, Anderson says that at the time the Horseshoe Tavern and the Flame Club in Minneapolis were the only two places in North America where you could play for an extended run. "It was one of those special places where you could sit down and play for one week, and not have to pack up every day," Anderson recalls. The country crooner would drive up from Nashville with his band (usually five or six strong) to play a week-long residency at Jack Starr's tavern. Often, they would play a gig somewhere else on the way to Toronto and then another en route back to Tennessee. Starr would put Anderson and his bandmates up at the Lord Simcoe Hotel. "I don't think I could have afforded that fine a hotel for me and my bandmates," Anderson jokes. Once located on the northeast corner of King Street and University Avenue, at 150 King Street West, the hotel opened in May 1957 and was closed in 1979, and the building was torn down in 1981.

Anderson remembers the Horseshoe as an intimate venue with a small stage. He always had a fairly big band. "We used to get creative on how to set up on the stage. The fans were right there in front of us and were always really responsive to our music. There was a country music station in town at the time, so they knew all our songs, applauded often, and sang along. The contract was for nightly shows from Wednesday to Saturday that included a matinee. These matinees," says Anderson, "saw kids come to the shows; they were always a family-friendly affair and a fun atmosphere."

In June 1965, the Country Music Hall of Famer went into the studio to cut a promising new song he wrote with bandmate Jimmy Gateley called "Bright Lights and Country Music." Anderson explains how the idea for the song came about:

> The ... idea came from a fan letter from a woman in London, Ontario, I got while out on the road. We were in Toronto working a little nightclub called the Horseshoe Tavern. We did a matinee on Saturday afternoon and a night show on Saturday night. One of my fans had written me a letter. She said, "I'm going to come to the night show because I like soft lights with my country music." I read the letter to Jimmy and both our ears perked up and our songwriters' antennas went up. We wrote almost the entire song in the dressing room at the Horseshoe Tavern.
>
> I told Jimmy, "There is an idea in here somewhere," but soft lights didn't feel right.

Throughout their whole set that night, the pair couldn't get the words from that letter out of their minds. When the show ended, they went down to the dressing room in the basement of the Horseshoe where, after each show, the fans would line up for autographs and pictures with the visiting Nashville musicians, shake hands, and buy records.

"On this night, we told the crowd to wait and be patient for a minute, as we had a song to write. They were very respectful and patient. With the door of our dressing room open, Jimmy and I, with our guitars, sat there, and the song came to life. It's the only song I ever wrote in front of an audience. We took turns coming up with lines and writing the tune," recalls Anderson.

Today, Anderson still lives in Music City and plays live every chance he gets. He also recently celebrated the fifty-fifth anniversary of his joining the Grand Ole Opry. "An old man like me doesn't need to be so busy!" he jokes. I catch up with the legendary country musician, and he tells me how he played the Horseshoe so many times over the years that the gigs all blend together. Still, he says there were a few shows that stood out for him.

One memorable night he unexpectedly received his first gold record. "I don't remember the year," he tells me, "but it was in the late 1960s. I had

The head of MCA Canada presents Whispering Bill Anderson (*right*) a gold record for *Bill Anderson's Greatest Hits*, onstage at the Horseshoe Tavern in May 1974.

been recording for Decca Records. Several of the local office staff in Toronto came down to the Horseshoe one night to see my performance. What I didn't know is they were there to present me with my first gold record. It was for my album *Bill Anderson's Greatest Hits*, which had gone gold in Canada. One of the guys from the record company came up on stage in the middle of our set and made the presentation. I still have the photo somewhere, and the framed record still hangs on my wall."

Like the other country music stars who played at the Horseshoe from the 1950s to the mid-1970s, Anderson recalls Starr as being a cordial and honest host. "He always honoured our contracts," he says.

The tavern owner and music promoter was also an avid golfer. He once tried to get Anderson to go tee it up with him, but for some reason that Anderson can't recall, the invitation to play a round together never panned out. Starr did drive Anderson up to CFGM, the country music station in Richmond Hill, for an interview once, though. Whisperin' Bill said he always enjoyed the candid conversations he had with the Horseshoe's original owner on those short trips.

*   *   *

In the mid 1960s, Starr hired Dick Nolan and the Blue Valley Boys (Johnny Burke, Roy Penney, and Bunty Petrie) as the Horseshoe's house band. They would play during the first part of the week, and then back up the Nashville headliners on the weekends.

Nolan was a pioneer of a Newfoundland style of country music, and was just nineteen when he brought that unique East Coast style to Toronto — first to the Drake Hotel, and later to the Horseshoe Tavern. By the time he died in 2005, Nolan had recorded forty albums and sold approximately one million records. He was the first Newfoundlander to have both a gold (fifty thousand units sold) and a platinum record (one hundred thousand units sold), and was also the first musician from The Rock to appear at the Grand Ole Opry. He's best known for his 1972 hit "Aunt Martha's Sheep."

When Nolan migrated to Toronto in 1958, he was set on seeing what the big city could offer. Before landing his first gig playing music, he waited tables at another country bar — the 300 Tavern at College and Spadina.

June Carter Cash and the Carter Family play the bar in the 1960s, when it was known as Nashville North, backed by the house band featuring lead guitarist Roy Penney.

Blue Valley Boy Roy Penney grew up with Nolan in Corner Brook, Newfoundland. The pair had been performing in several of the bars in their hometown before they were even of legal drinking age. Penney says during his stint at the Horseshoe in the mid-1960s, the Nashville musicians took him into their inner circle. He made fast friends with many of them, including the Carter Family, Little Jimmy Dickens, Billy Walker, and Charley Pride. They respected his hard work and dedication.

To prepare for each week's gigs, Penney would stay up late listening to the latest country and western hits on CFGM radio and capturing them with his trusty tape recorder so that he could play them back and learn the guitar licks. Many nights, if he didn't go to Aunt Bea's after-hours club or the Matador, he would drive the stars back to the Executive Hotel, where most of them stayed during their time in Toronto. Sometimes they would invite him up to their rooms and he would go and share a drink and chat about music. One night, Little Jimmy Dickens gave Penney a sneak preview of one of his new songs. It was a silly number called "May the Bird of Paradise Fly Up Your Nose." Well, that song went on to be a huge hit for Dickens,

Jack Starr (*far left*) poses next to famed Grand Ole Opry star and hillbilly singer Little Jimmy Dickens.

reaching number one on the country charts and number fifteen on the pop charts. Penney felt privileged to have been able to hear it first. For a good many years, the Horseshoe Tavern was the centre of Penney's life. Today, it's where his warmest memories still reside.

From 1963 to 1967, New Brunswick native Johnny Burke (née Jean Paul Bourque) played with Penney as the Blue Valley Boys' bassist. Burke was playing the New Shamrock Hotel at Coxwell and Gerrard when Nolan came to the club to hear him perform one night. After his set, Nolan asked Burke to join the band. The catch: they wanted the guitarist to play bass, which he had never played before. "I told them, 'I don't even know how to hold one!'" Burke says. "They replied, 'We can teach you pretty quick.'" So Burke borrowed his bass player's instrument and went to the Drake Hotel for an audition. A few fumbled notes surely occurred, but somehow the musician pulled it off. He was a Blue Valley Boy.

The next thing you knew, Starr hired Burke and the rest of the band — luring them away from their regular gig at the Drake by offering them each the union scale of $110 per week. "That was really good money in those days, because before I got into music, I was working in a silkscreen printing shop for forty dollars a week, working ten hours a day, six days a week," Burke recalls. "At the Horseshoe we did three, and later four, forty-five-minute sets a night, from 9:00 to 1:00, six days a week."

The Blue Valley Boys had Sundays off, but for the rest of the week they backed every Nashville act who came through town: from legends and Grand Ole Opry mainstays like Bill Anderson, Conway Twitty, Little Jimmy Dickens, Stonewall Jackson, George Hamilton IV, Tex Ritter, and Ferlin Husky to the new breed of burgeoning 1960s outlaw country acts, Waylon Jennings and Willie Nelson. Burke remembers when Tex Ritter appeared one Saturday night; the lineup on Queen Street stretched for several blocks — all the way down to Peter Street.

The local country and western fans made the Nashville artists feel right at home in Canada; the Horseshoe was one of the most welcoming venues they played on the touring circuit, which included stops at places like the Golden Nugget in Las Vegas and the Palomino Club in Los Angeles. George Hamilton IV was a regular at the bar; he especially loved Canadians, and playing the Queen Street tavern was always a treat. He sums it up in the liner notes to *Canadian Pacific*, the 1969 tribute album to his northern neighbour that features covers of songs written by Canadian folksingers such as Gordon Lightfoot and Joni Mitchell:

> Toronto is one of the great cities of the world and one of my truly "special places." (Along with Winston-Salem and Nashville.) It's becoming quite a booming music center and is even often referred to in country-music circles as the Nashville of the North. Two network Canadian country-music shows originate in Toronto (*The Tommy Hunter Show* and *Carl Smith's Country Music Hall*) and there are several clubs in the area that feature country music fulltime and a twenty-four-hour a day country music station — CFGM.

Another anecdote from Burke's four-year 'Shoe run involves Little Jimmy Dickens: "One afternoon Jimmy [Dickens] came in, and the fiddle player was playing a fiddle tune and I was playing bass just with my left hand, and I was hitting the snare drum with my right hand. Little Jimmy said, 'I like that!' so I played the whole week with him that way, which was a pain in the ass!"

Dottie West, who, along with Loretta Lynn and Patsy Cline, is considered one of country music's most influential female artists of all time, also played the Horseshoe. West arrived at the tavern in 1964, bringing with her the top ten hit "Love Is No Excuse" she had just recorded with Jim Reeves (who died tragically later that year in a plane crash). Burke recalls, "[West] asked me to learn Jim Reeves's part. Every time she came to play the Horseshoe, I did Reeves's part on that song with Dottie, which was a thrill."

Another night, the band who was appearing at the Horseshoe (their name escapes Burke all these years later) happened to have their set scheduled right in the middle of a Stanley Cup playoff game. Montreal was playing Toronto. Burke and the Horseshoe house band played a set before the game started, but by the time the headliners were set to start things up, the puck was dropping in the good ol' hockey game. The crowd protested; they wanted to watch the game. So, naturally, the musicians put down their instruments, sat with the rest of the audience, and watched the Maple Leafs battle the Canadiens on the one little TV that was perched in the corner over the bar. "If you couldn't see it, you would just wait for the screams," Burke recalls.

In 1967, Burke left the Blue Valley Boys and formed East Wind; the new band had a couple of appearances at the Horseshoe as the guest of the week in the early 1970s. While he hasn't played at the Horseshoe since those dying embers of the club's country music days burned, the East Coast musician hasn't stopped playing — he still plays with East Wind today. He's also been inducted into both the Canadian Country Music Hall of Fame and the New Brunswick Country Music Hall of Fame.

Fellow New Brunswick musician Norma Gallant later filled the vacancy Burke left in the 'Shoe's house band. Gallant had moved to the Big Smoke in the 1960s to pursue a music career, changing her name to Norma Gale — she was yet another travelling musician and East Coast migrant who found a temporary home at Toronto's Horseshoe Tavern.

Of all the East Coast migrants who found success and called the Horseshoe home, no one left more of a legacy or set more records than Mr. Charles Thomas Connors, better known as "Stompin' Tom." "If you ever had to put one thing in a time capsule to explain the Horseshoe, Stompin' Tom would be the one thing I would put in," says journalist Peter Goddard. In the next chapter, you will learn how and why this man from Skinners Pond, Prince Edward Island, came to define the next era in the legendary bar's history.

3

Tom's Stompin' Grounds

Come all you big drinkers, and sit yourself down
The Horseshoe Tavern waiters will bring on the rounds
There's songs to be sung
And stories to tell
Here at the hustlin'
Down at the bustlin'
Here at the Horseshoe Hotel
— Stompin' Tom Connors, "Horseshoe Hotel Song," from the gold
record *Live at the Horseshoe* (1971)

DRIFTER, OUTSIDER, LARGER-THAN-LIFE, and patriotic to the core — there was no one else like Stompin' Tom Connors.

Many consider the musician to have been a national treasure. His catchy songs with simple lyrics, which are easy to memorize, are still sung from coast to coast by generations of Canadians. Who doesn't know the refrains to his timeless tunes such as "Sudbury Saturday Night," "Bud the Spud," or "Big Joe Mufferaw," about everyday characters who embody the spirit of our country? Mark Starowicz captured the essence of Tom's patriotism in a feature for the *Last Post* in 1971:

> I never thought that nationalism was so deeply ingrained in this country until the first time I saw Connors at the Horseshoe. I've seen a packed crowd go wild over a singer before, but I've never, never seen so much unrestrained joy and applause as when this rumpled Islander got up and started strumming.

Jack Starr (*left*) celebrates with Stompin' Tom Connors on the occasion of the Horseshoe Tavern's twenty-fifth anniversary in 1972.

As the 1960s started to set, making way for the 1970s, the country singer from Skinners Pond, Prince Edward Island, made up his mind that he wanted to perform at the Horseshoe regularly. So he kept coming in and asking Starr to give him a chance. Again and again he'd get his courage up, only to have it knocked down by Starr. But eventually the young musician's persistence paid off. Jack Starr saw something others didn't in the fellow outsider.

Today, Connors's legacy is as legendary as the tavern itself. You could say, for a while, it became Tom's bar. "Tom made a big mark in that place," recalls Johnny Burke.

As this chapter unfolds, it will become clear that those eight words of Burke's are definitely an understatement. Dick Nolan's biographer, Wayne Tucker, shares the following anecdote that foreshadows Connors's lasting legacy:

> Willie Nelson played the Horseshoe in the 1960s, backed up by the Nolan-led Blue Valley Boys. Dick was around Willie every night and they raised a few glasses together.

The Blue Valley Boys — circa mid-1960s — who were the house band at the Horseshoe, backing up all the Grand Ole Opry stars. *From left:* Roy Penney, Bunty Petrie, Dick Nolan, Johnny Burke.

One particular time Dick and Willie were chatting over a beer while another performer who was an unknown at the time was on stage. Dick noticed Willie's mind was drifting and he kept looking up at the singer. Willie said, "Dick, that guy's got somethin' goin' for him. He's gonna turn out to be somebody."

And "somethin' goin' for him" he sure did have. Stompin' Tom went on to set attendance records at the 'Shoe that still stand today, more than forty years on. He recorded a gold record (*Live at the Horseshoe*) and filmed a feature concert film (*Across This Land with Stompin' Tom Connors*) in the bar's cozy confines, and his record of playing the bar for twenty-five consecutive nights is one that is likely never to be broken. Journalist Peter Goddard, who covered many of the musicians and shows at 370 Queen Street West starting in the early 1970s, provides his take on Tom's Horseshoe legacy: "If anybody could be said to embody the old and the new, the punk of the Horseshoe, it was Stompin' Tom. He was louder than any punk band. He came at you like a sledgehammer, which was perfect for the place. He was the real thing.… He also foreshadowed a lot of the punk bands that later tried to emulate him. If the Horseshoe ever reached the nadir of its identity it would be with him."

Connors's legacy was solidified at Starr's tavern. As with many Canadian musicians who came after him, the Horseshoe helped boost his career. "These people really like you, Tom," Jack Starr told Stompin' Tom in 1969, one year after Starr gave Connors his first gig. Those genuine words of gratitude came only after Canada's version of the outlaw country singer — who did not fit the mould of the Grand Ole Opry stars who had graced the stage over the previous decade — had proven his worth and gained the Horseshoe owner's admiration.

The late 1960s ushered in a new era at the Horseshoe Tavern, and Stompin' Tom led the charge. Like Starr, Tom was an outsider. Bands had a hard time keeping up with his stompin' foot and his offbeat rhythms. His songs spoke of blue-collar characters: drifters and dreamers like him. That's why his stompin' sounds and often silly sing-a-long lyrics resonated with the Horseshoe's loyal patrons, since the majority of Starr's regulars came from Connors's corner of the world: Atlantic Canada. Beyond his fellow East Coasters, Tom would draw a diverse crowd, a motley mix of beer-drinking regulars — from Toronto Maple Leafs fans, to college students, factory workers, and farmhands, to plainclothes police officers. Tom would sing a corny song filled with off-rhymes about Kirkland Lake, Sudbury, or another rural Ontario town, and the Horseshoe's patrons would holler, hoot, and pound the tables.

"Tom created a conversation," recalls Mickey Andrews, who played pedal steel with the Canadian icon for years. "He would always have a song about a town that someone from the audience could relate to. He had a different way of entertaining them, drawing out their animal instincts. They weren't rowdy, but they were boisterous, and the air was electrifying."

Stompin' Tom Connors got his moniker due to his penchant for pounding the floor with his cowboy boot, keeping time. These stomps were so heavy that they started to wear out the carpet and floorboards everywhere he performed. Eventually, Tom came up with the idea to put down a piece of plywood — a stompin' board, which he bought at Beaver Lumber — down on the stage before each show. As he stomped, dust and chips flew into the air. This was all part of the legend in the making.

Stompin' Tom Connors — who still holds the record for the most consecutive nights played at the Horseshoe Tavern — seen here in a still photo from the movie *Across This Land*.

The country singer from Canada's smallest province came to the club owners and concert promoters like a thirsty lion, not a shy lamb. Tom was always his own best PR person; the way he landed the gig at the Horseshoe is a perfect example of this dogged determination. Andrews recalls seeing Tom play at an after-hours club before Starr hired him, and thought he was tipping off the club owner to a new act. Not so. Tom had already gathered up his courage and been to see Starr many times, begging for a chance to play that storied stage. In late 1968, Starr finally relented, giving Connors a chance to prove himself by booking him for a one-week stint. It's something the late musician never forgot. In his memoir *Stompin' Tom and the Connors Tone*, the singer devotes an entire chapter, "Landing the Horseshoe," to Starr's bar. In it, Connors recalls the seminal moment when he signed his first contract to play the iconic institution on Queen:

> On the twenty-eighth or twenty-ninth of November, I got my courage up again and decided to go down to Toronto and try the Horseshoe Tavern, only this time minus the suit.

I really didn't have much faith in landing a job there because
the Horseshoe was known all over Canada. Everybody who
was a country fan and who landed in Toronto for any reason, either by plane, car, bus or train, for any length of time,
sooner or later, wound up paying a visit to the Horseshoe.
The owner's name was Jack Star [*sic*] and he had kept the
place "country" through thick and thin now for over twenty
years and the club had a great reputation. There wasn't hardly
a weekend that went by that the place wasn't packed, due
mainly to the fact that he would always bring a big-name
act from Nashville, Tennessee, to play Friday and Saturday
night. When Jack finally arrived on the scene I was pleas-
antly surprised to find that he was a very quiet, congenial
man, even though he had the demeanour of a person who
knew his business very well. He made me feel at ease and
I began telling him what I had done, where I had been up
until now, and just how much I wanted a chance to play his
club to see how well I could fare. "Well," he said, "I'm trying
out a new house band next week and if you want to come in
and see if they can back you up, I'll give you the opportunity
to see what you can do. Bring your contract in before you
start on Monday night and I'll sign you on for a week.

Tom could not believe his ears. That weekend he went back to where
he was staying, and that's all he could talk about with the owners of the
house. On Monday, at around four o'clock in the afternoon, he returned to
the Horseshoe and just sat there for the next five hours, until his set time at
9:00 p.m. The only interruption to his thoughts came when Starr stopped
by his table and asked him for his union contract. After signing it, Starr
shook Connors's hand and said, "You must really want to play here. I've been
watching you sit there for the last three or four hours, and I don't think you
took your eyes off the stage once."

That first gig established the tone and set up Tom for his legendary run
at the Horseshoe. Tom was relaxed and ready to give it his best shot. "This
gig is going to be a snap for me," he said, "because every place [I] had ever
played up until now, [I] had to carry the whole ball all by [myself]." At other

bars, Tom was used to starting at 8:00 p.m. instead of 9:00, and he would do four one-hour sets, with only a fifteen-minute break after each hour, before finishing up at 1:00 a.m. At the 'Shoe, he had to play for only an hour and a half during the whole night.

From the time he dropped his famed stompin' board on the stage and started to sing, he never looked back. Initially, the boys in the house band found it difficult to keep time with Tom, but as soon as they realized his left heel was always coming down on the offbeat, rather than on the downbeat, they quickly grasped what was going on and started to have almost as much fun watching Tom as the audience did. Connors recalls the reaction on that memorable night: "Even the waiters who had been there for twenty years or more were seen from time to time to just be standing there wondering how in the hell could I stand on one foot for so long and go through the antics I did without falling down."

In between sets, Tom used the time to do what he did best: public relations — consuming a beer at every table, talking to everyone, and selling his records. By the time the night was over, the musician knew every patron by his or her first name; he then stood by the front door, as if he owned the place, thanking them for coming as they left.

By the end of that first week, word had spread along Queen Street and out into the suburbs. Many people came back to see the show on the weekend and brought their friends. Even though the place still wasn't packed, Stompin' Tom managed to get another contract signed with Starr — this time not just for one week, but for three.

For Tom, the chance Starr gave him that November and the faith he placed in him was the best gift he ever received. It's also one he never forgot. "This all took place about the first week of December in 1968," he recalls in his memoir. "It gave me the extra money I needed to buy Christmas presents for everybody, but the best Christmas present of all was the one I got. And that was my opportunity to play the Horseshoe Tavern in Toronto for the first time."

The following February, Tom returned to the Horseshoe, backed by a new house band. Apparently Jack Starr was trying out different bands at that time, trying to find one he was happy to hire full-time. That return to the 'Shoe for Tom was not what he had expected, because he didn't click with this band as he had with the one he had played with the previous November. Connors reflects on this lack of chemistry:

From my very first night on the stage, I could see the guys in this band were either very jealous of me, or they just didn't appreciate what I was trying to do. I was singing my own songs, of course, and doing absolutely nothing from the current hit parade. This they didn't seem to understand. For the whole week they didn't talk to me and just kept screwing up my songs whenever they could in an effort to discourage me and get me to quit. During each break they'd just go to a back table and sit by themselves while I was always associating with the people. And practically every table I went to, they'd tell me how the band kept sneering, laughing and pointing at me behind my back in an effort to get the audience to do the same thing. Unfortunately for them, their little scheme wasn't working. I just ignored the whole thing, did the best I could under the circumstances, and kept right on with my public relations.

At the end of Saturday's matinee, Starr called Tom into his office and asked him how he liked the new band and how they were getting along. Connors, ever diplomatic when he needed to be, knowing how tough it sometimes was for musicians to get work and not wanting to lessen their chances of keeping their jobs in any way, told Starr that while they did seem to be a bit standoffish, it was probably due to shyness, and while they hadn't quite caught on to his music yet, they would probably get used to him and do a lot better job next week.

Starr wasn't fooled. He knew the truth. The tavern owner replied, "Well, Tom, that's all very decent of you, but you don't have to give me any crap. These guys have been into my office three times this week trying to get me to let you go. They said you can't keep steady rhythm, you're annoying the customers, and your foot is driving them crazy."

As Starr sat staring at him from behind his desk, Tom tried to defend himself against these allegations. Before long, Jack interrupted him and eased his mind: "Don't worry yourself about it. I've been keeping tabs on the whole situation, and after tonight, you won't have to work with these guys anymore. I'm keeping you and letting them go."

Starr then asked Tom how he had gotten along with the previous band he had played with. Tom told Jack he thought they were excellent and that they had all gotten along very well. The good news was that Starr still had that band on standby, and he assured Tom they'd be backing him up the following week and any time he played the Horseshoe thereafter. Then Starr flashed his infectious smile, got up from his desk, shook Tom's hand, and said, "These people really like you, Tom. Now go and get 'em."

That band that Tom played with when he returned to the 'Shoe the following Monday had just seen Clint Eastwood's latest western *The Good, the Bad and the Ugly* and decided it was a perfect moniker for their trio: Cape Bretoners Mickey Andrews on pedal steel and bassist Randy MacDonald, along with Newfoundlander Gerry Hall on lead guitar. These three musicians were the Horseshoe's regular house band up until the mid 1970s, shortly before Starr retired from the business in 1976.

In those days, the Horseshoe could seat between 300 and 350 people. By Tom's third week of regular gigs, the place was packed even before the Nashville guests arrived on Saturday night. Most of the customers were from Newfoundland or the Maritimes, but Tom started to draw lots of patrons from all over Ontario and from western Canada. Tom continued his public relations each and every night. As well as stopping to chat at every table, he would often hold short conversations with patrons from the stage, especially if he hadn't seen them there before. It was all part of his attempt to break down any barriers that might have existed between artist and audience, creating a familial atmosphere that still exists today at the tavern. Connors would introduce these newbies to the people sitting at the next table, and before you knew it they were pulling their tables together and acting as if they had known each other all their lives. As Tom says in his memoir, "This encouraged people to be friendlier toward one another and made them feel like we were all just one big happy family. This also made the jobs of the waiters much easier and reduced the incidents of trouble to practically nil."

In the second week of May 1969, Tom was back at the Horseshoe for another five-week stint. This run eventually doubled, becoming ten. His legend was growing. Ever the PR man, Tom did his part. At each show before the band took the stage, he would place two or three free books of matches at each table as an added courtesy. As it was too expensive to have his name printed on the outside of the covers, he had a rubber stamp made and gave the kids of the family where he was living at the time a few bucks to stamp them all. The design on the stamp was the same as the picture of the guitar on the sides of his truck. The words read "Hometown Songs by Stompin' Tom."

"Altogether I must have doled out about nine or ten thousand books of matches during the full ten weeks I was there," Tom recalls in his memoir. "They not only provided a convenience, but a lot of people just took them home for souvenirs. This was also another method of promoting myself in a rather inexpensive way."

Mickey Andrews, Tom's long-time pedal steel player, recalls another way Tom promoted himself. "One of biggest things Tom did [and] he didn't even tell us, is he spent all his money on these big billboards around Toronto that would say *Help Stamp Out Stompin' Tom*. You didn't know how to take it. I eventually found out it cost him seven hundred dollars for each one of these ads, but it created a big thing about him because they wouldn't play him on the radio … no matter how hard he tried in those days, he couldn't get airplay. They wanted their music to sound like what it sounded like in Nashville."

Radio play obviously didn't matter to this new generation of Horseshoe patrons, who couldn't care less whether Tom sounded like he came from the Grand Ole Opry. By the end of Tom's third week at the 'Shoe, the tavern was beginning to be just as packed on the weeknights as it was on the weekends. This was when Jack Starr approached the singer and asked what other booking commitments he had lined up when his current five weeks were done at the Horseshoe. He said he was prepared to double Tom's wages and that the musician could stay as long as he wanted. That meant Connors would be making twice as much working for Starr as he would anywhere else. The decision was easy. Tom cancelled a couple of smaller venues and ended up working for Jack for an additional five weeks. This stretch of ten straight weeks for a single featured performer and twenty-five consecutive nights in a row became the official record of endurance that still stands today. Eventually, he got bigger than the Nashville acts because he drew a bigger crowd, not because he had more hit songs. Two other records Tom still holds from the old Horseshoe are for the most patrons and the biggest turnover in any one week, and the most patrons and biggest turnover in any one Saturday. Stonewall Jackson previously held the last record, for Saturdays. The North Carolinian honky-tonker, whose 1959 million-selling hit "Waterloo" kicked off a successful career that lasted for more than a decade, was a regular fixture on the Opry — and at the 'Shoe — during the 1960s. For those wondering, his ancestry does draw a line back to the famous Confederate Civil War general of the same name. The night Tom broke Jackson's record, he was performing with The Good, the Bad and the Ugly and people were lined up three and four deep, halfway down the block.

It was at the Horseshoe where Tom met a young man from Canadian Music Sales Corporation. He listened to Tom's songs, liked what he heard, and invited the young musician to join him for a beer. The man was Jury Krytiuk, from Melfort, Saskatchewan, and he had recently been appointed head of CMS's small record label Dominion Records. A deal was inked. By 1972, Tom had recorded a number of albums for the Dominion label, including a box set called *Stompin' Tom Connors Sings 60 Old Time Favourites*, containing five LPs. By now, songs like "Bud the Spud," and "Sudbury Saturday Night" were synonymous with Stompin' Tom; everybody knew those songs.

Steve Fruitman was one of those early Connors converts. When he was growing up in Timmins, Ontario, Steve used to listen to Tom's daily radio program *Live from the Skyway Room at the Maple Leaf Hotel* over CKGB. Tom became somewhat of a hero to Steve. After he left Timmins, Steve lost track of Connors's career until one day, after watching *Hockey Night in Canada* (which used to end when the game was over, and then CBC would switch to the program already in progress), he caught an episode of *Countrytime* with Vic Mullen from Halifax, Nova Scotia. He explains:

> I wasn't really into country music back then, in 1968, but I kind of liked it. It was basically the only music we had to listen to up north because "our music," rock music, could only be heard late at night during the *Hilltop Rendezvous* program on the French station, CFCL. So out comes this special guest star dressed in a black leather vest, big cowboy boots and a hat and a board to beat his heel into and he sings, "*Twang twang, a diddle dang a diddle danga — twang twanga diddle dang another dang twang,*" and I said, "That's the guy from Timmins!"

After moving to Toronto, the teenaged Steve was a regular at the Horseshoe, singing along with the rest of the tavern's faithful to all of Tom's songs about characters and places he'd seen in his rambles following the white line. Fruitman, being underage, had been sneaking into the Horseshoe as an eighteen-year-old. When he turned nineteen, the Ontario provincial government of Bill Davis lowered the drinking age from twenty-one to eighteen. He recalls those unforgettable nights: "I'd go to the 'Shoe with my school friends, get a good seat, which was a difficult thing to do even on a weeknight, and get right into it. I purchased my first Stompin' Tom album, *Bud the Spud*, at the Horseshoe and got Tom to stomp on the cover (having removed the record first). For a kid into The Who, early Led Zeppelin, and stuff like that, this was rather different indeed."

*   *   *

Flash ahead to December 1972: Tom and The Good, the Bad and the Ugly returned to the Horseshoe. This time, it was for a very special occasion; it had been twenty-five years since Jack Starr had opened his storied tavern. The house that Jack built had grown from a beer and whisky bar, known for its roast beef dinners, to the top country and western venue in the country. It was time to celebrate this milestone, and of course Stompin' Tom figured into the party. Along with banners flying and hundreds of patrons coming and going all week, wishing the Tavern well, Stompin' Tom sang the "Horseshoe Hotel Song" several times every night. This was one of the songs included on the *Live at the Horseshoe* album he had recorded in the bar the previous year. "It was sure getting a workout on an occasion as special as this," Tom recalled in his memoir *Stompin' Tom and the Connors Tone.*

On the Saturday night of the week-long celebration, the place was hopping. The stage was decorated with wreaths and flowers, and Jack went up to receive some well-deserved accolades, take a few pictures, and give a speech. Jack regaled the patrons with stories of the Horseshoe's humble beginnings, including how he'd missed by only one day obtaining the very first liquor licence ever awarded in Toronto. Starr also reminisced about the good times and some of the bad, and name-dropped a few of the great country stars that had performed on the Horseshoe stage. Then, out of nowhere, at least according to Stompin' Tom, Starr came out with this proclamation: "Ladies and gentlemen, of all the great entertainers that ever played on this stage, the one that jingled my till the most, the one who broke all previous attendance records and set new ones, the guy who came from nowhere and surprised all of us, and the guy we love because he sings all those songs that make us proud to be Canadian, is none other than this young man standing right here: Stompin' Tom Connors."

You would think that after such a remark the crowd would go crazy and take the roof off the place. Well, they did. Tom waved and took a bow, and while he was acknowledging his fans Jack reached into a box he was carrying and pulled out a framed gold record for his *Live at the Horseshoe* album, passing it to the singer, who was still stunned. "This is one you never expected, Tom, and all the gang from Dominion Records and Boot Records asked me if I'd present it to you, and I'm more than happy to do so," said Starr. "And whatever you do, Tom, just keep on stompin'."

No sooner had Starr uttered the word "stompin'" than everyone in the Horseshoe started to do just that. As Tom tried to say thank you to everyone who had bought the record and helped to make the gold album possible, several people dumped some pretty stiff drinks into his water jug that he usually kept on stage, and some of it spilled into the flowers. The press took a couple of pictures of Starr and Stompin' Tom with the gold album propped up in front of them, and afterward the pair answered a few questions, then left the stage.

Later, after another short set, Stompin' Tom and Starr wished everybody a merry Christmas. Everyone in the Horseshoe Tavern raised their glasses, gave a toast to their host and their hometown musical hero, and drank up. With that, another chapter in the tavern's history closed. What would the next twenty-five years hold in store? More outsiders like Starr and Connors — all fuelled by the same passion for the music and for keeping Starr's bar alive for another generation to enjoy and discover.

* * *

In 1973, Tom left one more mark on the Horseshoe Tavern before bidding goodbye to this phase of his career. The film *Across This Land with Stompin' Tom Connors*, directed by John Saxton and featuring a young University of Toronto student named David Cronenberg as an assistant production manager, stands as a time capsule. The film, produced and distributed by Montreal schlock studio Cinépix, captures the quintessential Canadian

Stompin' Tom Connors pictured in the movie *Across This Land*, which was filmed at the Horseshoe Tavern in 1974.

country singer at his best, in the place where he first found success. The PR team Cinépix used to generate awareness and excitement for the movie came up with the following unique selling proposition: *There's a bit of country in all of us, just waitin' to bust loose.* The feature-length music documentary was filmed mostly at the 'Shoe. This wasn't Tom's first foray into film, having made his screen debut the previous year in *This Is Stompin' Tom*, a short film that wove interview segments into performance footage.

In *Across This Land*, cowboys and cowgirls sit at tables that crowd the stage. They swig beer, hoot and holler, and stomp along to every song. Tom is at his storytelling best, regaling the audience with the inspiration behind each song. Many guests join Tom on the stage, which features a prominent wagon wheel and artwork designed by amateur artist John Anthony Cullen that reads "The Horseshoe Tavern: The Home of Country Music." The film kicks things off with a rousing version of "Sudbury Saturday Night" before Connors spends the next ninety minutes telling Newfie jokes and belting out some of his biggest hits, including "Bud the Spud," "Big Joe Mufferaw," and "Rubberhead," as well as parodies of Nashville standards like "Green, Green Grass of Home" and "Muleskinner Blues" (all of which he later released as a live double LP on his own Boot Records). Occasionally, the set list is broken up by guest performances by the likes of Kent Brockwell, Sharon Lowness, Chris Scott, Bobby Lalonde, and Joey Tardif. As each performs, Tom leaves the stage, joins a table of patrons in the front row, and has a couple of beers with his fans.

* * *

In 1961, Michael T. Wall arrived in Toronto from Corner Brook, Newfoundland. Like Stompin' Tom and many fellow Maritimers, Wall came to the Big Smoke looking for work. Before finding success as a country music singer, songwriter, and musician, he worked at a variety of odd jobs, including picking tobacco in Concord, Ontario. "I had a dream to promote my province to the world, and I have done that," Wall says. He certainly has achieved that dream. He's promoted Newfoundland from Australia to Asia and all parts in between over the past fifty years. He admits it's been a bumpy road at times, but says if you love it, it's important, and the one constant in his life is that he's always loved country music. Johnny Cash was Wall's hero: "When I first heard him in 1956, I said that's what I want to do."

Today, people refer to Wall as "ageless Michael T." At seventy-eight, the Canadian Country Music Hall of Fame member continues to bring his unique brand of country music to the world. The first time Wall performed at the Horseshoe was in 1968. Later, he became the singing host at the Molly and Me Tavern and Nightclub at Bloor and Lansdowne. "The place was jam-packed every weekend," Wall recalls. "I was there for eight and a half years as the host. Sometimes some Nashville stars like Charley Pride would come to watch my show."

"For a long time, I would sneak in the back door of the Horseshoe to see all the Nashville stars," Wall recalls. "One night Jack [Starr] caught me and said, 'You go around front and pay like everybody else.' So, I did from then on."

Charley Pride, RCA Victor's "Pride of Country Music," holds court and signs autographs at the Horseshoe Tavern's coat check during his first Canadian visit in 1967.

Once Starr found out Wall could also play and sing, he booked the Newfoundlander. "Jack booked people whom he knew would draw," Wall says. "He knew I would draw because the Newfoundlanders would come out in busloads to support me. The Maritimers supported me from day one, and they are still supporting me. They wanted to hear a little bit of Newfoundland in Toronto."

If you got a chance to sing at the Horseshoe Tavern, says Wall, it was special, since Mr. Starr booked only the best entertainers from both sides of the border: "I was privileged to appear there many times, singing my own brand of Canadian country music."

Besides playing the Horseshoe, Wall was privileged to meet and rub shoulders with Nashville stars like Bill Anderson, Little Jimmy Dickens, Tommy Hunter, Tommy Cash (Johnny's younger brother), the Carter Family, the Stoneman Family, Skeets McDonald, and bluegrass legend Jimmy Martin.

* * *

Born in 1939 in Trout River, Newfoundland, Roy Payne never knew his father. All he knew was that his dad played the fiddle, so there must have been some musical gene in there somewhere. Raised by his grandmother, Payne later learned his real mother was someone he had always thought was his sister. With no parental figure to guide him, Payne left home and school early, hitting the road. First, he was trained as a chainsaw mechanic; then, at seventeen, after a night fuelled by booze, Payne joined the army — spending a dozen years as a soldier, serving with peacekeeping forces in Egypt and Cypress. His final stop was at Canadian Forces Base Borden in Barrie, Ontario, where he was discharged. While serving his country, in his limited free time Payne wrote songs for fun. After leaving the army, he got a job as a chauffeur to Member of Provincial Parliament Darcy McKeough. Riding around in what he dubbed "the big Chrysler," he wrote a ton of songs. Payne once claimed to a reporter that he had written about 2,600 songs over the course of fifteen years.

Like Michael T. Wall, even before landing a regular gig at Starr's bar, Payne frequented the Horseshoe. While he was in the army, on his days off he would visit the tavern on his weekend leaves to watch Dick Nolan and his band perform. Later, he attended the matinees on Saturdays to sing a song or two. From watching the house band and sitting in with them, before he knew it, Payne's name, too, was in lights and posters on Queen Street. Though Payne had little professional experience and very few shows under his belt, for some reason Starr, as he did with Stompin' Tom, took a chance on Payne, giving him a featured booking. There was something in the way the young man sang and played that Starr knew would resonate with his patrons, especially those from the East Coast. Before he knew it, Payne was headlining the hallowed bar as the leader of the Horseshoe's house band, which included Terry Hall, Marie Battam, Randy McDonald, and Mickey Andrews, who had played pedal steel for Stompin' Tom for many years.

For nearly five years in the 1970s Payne would play with the band for seven-week stints, head out on the road for a while, and then come back and play the tavern again. Payne remained friends with Dick Nolan and collaborated with him on occasion; he wrote the liner notes and title song to Nolan's 1974 album *Happy Anniversary Newfoundland*.

Payne's best-known hit was "Goofy Newfie," at one time the most requested song on CFGM. The album went on to sell close to five hundred thousand copies. Payne wrote this song — his first ever recording — at the Horseshoe, bragging he penned the composition in less than five minutes.

Michael T. Wall, "The Singing Newfoundlander," with fellow Newfies Roy Payne and Reg Watkins — all of whom played the Horseshoe Tavern many times in the early to mid-1970s.

Starr was impressed with Payne's blue-collar poetry and ended up signing Payne to a contract, paying the songwriter approximately five hundred dollars. According to Payne, several months later Starr sold this contract to RCA Records for a lot more money. It's something the musician never forgot. While he was grateful to Jack for taking a chance on him, he felt a little cheated by this business deal. Payne described this situation to John Gavin: "He just signed me to negotiate a contract with RCA and he had all the money in the world. I'll never forget that and they say he is dead now. I wonder did he take it all with him. I always had a saying that I acquired years ago, that I believe in: I saw a lot of things, but I never seen a Brinks Truck chase a hearse, that's true, so you can't take it with you."

Budgeting was not Payne's forte. He certainly lived life with the credo "Spend today, for tomorrow you may die." The following quote, as told to Blaik Kirby of the *Globe and Mail* in June 1974, sums up Payne's philosophy when it came to dollar bills:

From left: Ed Preston, President of RCA Records Canada, with fellow employees Scott Richards and Johnny Murphy, along with Grand Ole Opry star George Hamilton IV.

Gordon Lightfoot (*left*) makes a surprise appearance at the Horseshoe Tavern on Ed Preston night, honouring RCA Victor's promo team, in the late 1960s.

When I started, all I really wanted was money, money, money. But all my friends were there because of the money. I'd rather be the way I am now, I make a good living, I'm quite contented, and while I've got to have money to live, it doesn't mean a damn thing. It doesn't come number one for me now.... It's feelings, not money, that counts. I wouldn't care if I died a pauper, so long as I could pass on to my kid my feelings.

*   *   *

Gary LeDrew moved to Ontario in 1947, the same year Jack Starr opened the Horseshoe Tavern, so it must have been fate that he would one day become connected to the venerable venue. Flash forward to 1974: A friend of LeDrew's owned an apartment across the street from the tavern, and the pair decided to turn the building into a speakeasy. Over the years, everyone from Roy Payne to Murray McLachlan and, later, many punk and new wave acts frequented his after-hours club. He set up drums, a microphone, speakers, and amps so that all the travelling musicians could play in his bar. The cops were aware of the place but often turned a blind eye, as they were regulars at the Horseshoe during the day and LeDrew had made friends with some of them. Often, LeDrew sported a big black cowboy hat; many folks mistook him for Ronnie Hawkins. He was a good-timin' man who liked the nightlife, so it comes as no surprise that during the day the Horseshoe became his local and, as a fellow club owner, he got his drinks for free. From sipping tea with Kitty Wells to hosting Mick Jagger at his after-hours club, LeDrew could tell stories about those Queen Street years for days. One particular story about Roy Payne stands out:

> Payne owed Morty [Starr] (who was running the day-to-day operations of the Horseshoe after his uncle Jack retired) $3,000 from unpaid bar bills. Morty let him play for the whole month of August to pay back this debt, but at the end of the month, due to Roy's fondness for liquid libations, Roy owed him $6,000!

After that, he made a deal with Morty that he wouldn't drink. Well, I met a couple of friends one afternoon at the Horseshoe. Morty was at the bar and Roy was setting up on stage. A little while later, I felt something grab my leg. It was Roy. He had crawled under all the booths and he whispered up to me "Get me a beer!" We became great friends after that.

LeDrew's after-hours club finally closed its doors in 1980.

* * *

In 1976, after more than twenty-eight years running the Horseshoe Tavern, Jack Starr was not quite ready to drift off into that good night, but he was finally ready to retire from day-to-day operations of the club. The ever-astute businessman didn't sell the name "Horseshoe Tavern." A lot of people wanted the moniker.

With Starr's retirement, those later years of the 1970s saw a slow erosion of the bar's loyal country patrons. Morty Starr's business acumen was not in the same league as his uncle's, and he didn't have the same connections to the older country stars. Looking to draw a new crowd, Morty started booking other musical acts that were outside the country and western genre — more jazz, folk, and blues-based sounds. Beyond new Canadian country-rock pioneers like Prairie Oyster, other performers at the Horseshoe from 1976 to 1978 included the likes of David Wilcox, a teenage Colin Linden, and Ken Whiteley's the Original Sloth Band.

Over a cup of tea at Whiteley's basement studio in Toronto, the seven-time Juno Award–winning roots musician recalls his early days playing the Horseshoe Tavern, with the likes of Wilcox, Linden, and Willie P. Bennett, but mainly with the Original Sloth Band. Whiteley, who grew up in Don Mills, Ontario, recalls going to the 'Shoe to watch some hot country cats like George Hamilton IV while he was still in high school. His trademark bushy beard, which he still sports today, certainly helped get him in. "In those days, if you looked like you might be old enough to drink and you carried yourself like you belonged, they didn't ask you for ID," he says. Some of the dates are fuzzy, but he cannot forget celebrating

Ken Whiteley (standing), with members of the Original Sloth Band, who played the venerable 'Shoe regularly in the mid-1970s.

his twenty-fifth birthday there in 1976: "I was playing with the Sloth Band, and my folks came to the gig." He remembers singing the classic Bessie Smith blues tune "Down in the Dumps," with lyrics apropos to the occasion.

At the time, the Sloth Band was booked at the Horseshoe weekly from Thursday to Saturday, including a weekend matinee. They played three sets a night, and Whiteley admits it was really good money: "By the late 1970s, we could make two thousand dollars for a weekend of gigs. We had a guaranteed contract and were not working for the door, which would become the new model by the end of the 1980s." Another memory from this period involves the Sloth Band's drummer, Bill Usher. "It was at the Horseshoe during one of our gigs in 1977 where Bill met Sharon, Lois and Bram, and started to plan their debut record."[*]

* * *

---

[*] Bill played on the Sloth Band's record *Hustlin' and Bustlin'*, recorded in the fall of 1975. He and Sharon, Lois and Bram already knew each other through the Mariposa In the Schools program and the annual Mariposa Folk Festival. They were in the audience that night in 1977, and chatted with Bill during the break. Whiteley says it may have been a pre-arranged meeting, but he can't recall for sure.

When it comes to the Horseshoe Tavern, Colin Linden can talk for hours and vividly recall and name date after date, starting in the late 1970s, every gig he's ever played there: from his headlining debut in 1977 to the night in December 1999, while he was performing with Blackie and the Rodeo Kings, when his good friend Rick Danko died, and many more memorable evenings. So many of the touchstones of the artist's life occurred inside the walls of 370 Queen Street West. It's the club of many firsts for the musician; it's where he cut his teeth as a young guitarist, honing his chops and confidence playing live as a sideman with the likes of Whiteley, Willie P. Bennett, and David Wilcox before taking the stage for his debut in November 1977. Linden was even served papers once while he was on the Horseshoe's stage by a lawyer who wanted to sue him, and he still bears a scar on the top of his head from a mishap diving off the stage back in 1984. "It was older than any of us and had this gravitas," the songwriter recalls. "There are so many things that happened in the dressing rooms downstairs and different places … it has a real mythology to it."

Linden recalls how he got his start playing at the 'Shoe:

> In 1977 I was seventeen and had just quit school, and encouraged largely by David Wilcox, I started my own band. I thought, *Okay, let's see if I can get a gig at the Horseshoe.* I went down and met with Peter Graham, who was booking the venue at the time. I had just cut my first demo and wanted to play it for him, so went down the big alley beside the club to Graham's car where I played my cassette for him. I knew where all the mistakes were on the demo, so I talked over all of them, and he hired me! On November 28, 1977, I started my first week as a band leader at the Horseshoe Tavern as Colin Linden and the Lucky Charms. It was just fantastic! I received reviews from all three Toronto papers. Playing the Horseshoe was the beginning of a lot of things for me. It was a huge confidence-builder. I was only seventeen, but since I was a union member they let me play bars as long as I didn't drink.

Whiteley and Linden — along with their style of roots music — were some of the last remnants of the Peter Graham booking era in the late seventies. By early 1978, the Horseshoe Tavern was ready for yet another change in direction. Enter the promoting pair, known as The Garys — Gary Topp and Gary Cormier — with their eclectic musical tastes and discerning ears for a new scene.

4

The Garys Shake Things Up

To me, punk is about being an individual and going against the grain
and standing up and saying, "This is who I am."
— Joey Ramone

IN THE MID- TO LATE 1970S the Horseshoe was still widely known as
a country bar, but since the retirement of original owner Jack Starr in 1976
the venue had been slowly losing its identity. Just like Toronto the Good at
the time, the Horseshoe badly needed a reinvention, a cultural revolution to
inject life into the well-weathered walls.

Cowboys and cowgirls who looked like they had just rolled in along
with the tumbleweeds from an Albertan ranch were still the 'Shoe's main
patrons. But impresarios Gary Topp and Gary Cormier, known as "The
Garys," quickly changed that, ushering in a new musical era. The cowpokes
were replaced by misfits, the cowgirls by punk rock girls dressed in skinny
jeans, leather jackets, and black or white T-shirts spray-painted with the
names of their favourite bands.

Nineteen seventy-eight was a watershed year in the Horseshoe's history.
Not only did it change ownership, with The Garys taking control of bookings,
but it also became a club with a higher purpose. As The Garys' inaugural concert poster proclaimed, "The Horseshoe: The First Concert Club in Toronto."
While it rattled the regulars, who lamented the end of a twenty-five-year tradition of country and western music, for those in the know, those eight months
from mid-March to early December when The Garys were given carte blanche
to book whomever they wanted, every night was a magical, memorable live
music experience. The Garys put up their own posters — both east and west

and north and south of Queen and Spadina. They would arrive at the bar at five o'clock in the afternoon and wouldn't leave until three the next morning. The Garys were going against the grain with a shared raison d'être.

"You didn't know what was going to happen," Gary Topp recalls. "You didn't know if there was going to be a fight, or whether the plumbing would flood … everybody was there for a purpose; there was an atmosphere that was irreplaceable."

Prior to taking over bookings at the Horseshoe, Gary Topp and Gary Cormier ran the New Yorker Theatre on Yonge Street, fifty yards south of where the underground indie cinema Cinecity once stood. At this popular theatre, the pair promoted shows, including the Ramones' first Toronto visit, curated movies like the Beatles' *Magical Mystery Tour* and *Yellow Submarine*, and hosted myriad art-themed nights. Topp had previously owned another movie house: the Original 99 Cent Roxy.

Many of the patrons of these establishments ended up forming punk bands that later played the Horseshoe. Gary Cormier had also managed bands like Rough Trade and Joe Hall and the Continental Drift, both of which had previously played the Horseshoe, which is how he got to know the manager at the time, Peter Graham.

The Garys (Gary Cormier and Gary Topp) booked the Horseshoe for a memorable eight months in 1978.

When Graham approached The Garys to take the venerable old tavern in a new direction, the bar was due for a change. Sales were slipping. The country fans were not as loyal to the old lady as they once had been.

The grande dame of Queen needed some fresh blood and bold ideas, and that's exactly what The Garys brought to the business. The pair had built up a loyal following at the New Yorker, but with rents climbing, the businessmen couldn't keep pace with the rising costs. It's no surprise they jumped at the chance to take their curatorial model that had won over a core audience at the New Yorker down to Queen West.

Working for eighteen hours straight, the first thing they did was move the stage from the middle of the west wall in the backroom, near where the current back bar is, to the the far end of the room on the north wall. Then they built up the stage to three feet, making it what they considered a proper height, and enclosed it with three walls. They brought in a new PA and lighting system, and installed a light and sound system as well as film projectors and overhead screens, video machines, and other gadgets.

As Cormier told Gary Toushek of the *Globe and Mail*, their intent was never to alienate the regulars:

> The Horseshoe is a genuine Queen Street bar made authentic by its clientele, the street people, the country and western fans. We're not out to destroy that, we're adding to it, changing it for what we hope will add enjoyment of the audience. We want to make the Horseshoe more than just a bar. We want to make it a cultural melting pot. New York has the Fillmore and CBGB — Toronto never really came close to the concept that these places offer.

The Garys also hung a horseshoe, embroidered by Cormier's wife, Martha, on the black backdrop of the stage. It would become the new insignia for the tavern. Like the horseshoe in their handbills, it was hung upside down — if the tines of a horseshoe are pointing down, it's supposed to be a bad sign, meaning its luck has run out. The backstory is that when these promoters first started booking concerts at the New Yorker, they gave out T-shirts that featured the New York skyline with a man holding a horseshoe as souvenirs to the bands who played there. Dee Dee Ramone even wore one of these shirts on the cover of their second album, *Leave Home*. This symbol was an omen, for sure, that The Garys' run would not last forever. Still, while it lasted, every night was an experience. You didn't know what was going to happen.

"You would turn your jeans inside out and sew them straight," recalls Lin Duperron, a regular patron during The Garys' tenure at the 'Shoe. "We bought leather jackets at surplus stores or real motorcycle jackets … we were budding musicians, artists, and writers; many of us didn't have a steady income, so it was a way for us to get creative."

While it's now remembered most as the Horseshoe's punk rock era — thanks largely to the documentary *The Last Pogo*, which chronicled the infamous last night of mayhem that was The Garys' swan song — during those 240 days, the promoters brought in an eclectic mix of the creative arts: everything from avant-garde jazz to reggae, singer-songwriters to blues, and even comedy with the likes of Darryl Rhoades and the Hahavishnu Orchestra. As the 'Shoe's new chief curators, the duo simply booked the bands they liked — either local or imported. Here's just a sampling of the performers who graced the venue's marquee that year: the Police, Sun Ra, Pere Ubu, Cecil Taylor, Etta James, Jesse Winchester, the Viletones, Suicide, the Stranglers, and the I Threes.

According to Topp, two of his most memorable shows were the Stranglers, for which around one thousand people (two hundred over capacity) were shoehorned into the place, and Pere Ubu, the first imported band the pair ever booked.

"We were very eclectic in our tastes and bringing in stuff that was in our record collections," Cormier says. "We booked people we thought were great that deserved to be shown in there."

The Last Pogo co-producer and director Colin Brunton had worked with Topp since his Roxy days, and was offered a job at the Horseshoe. The job description was vague:

"Do you want me to bus tables?"

"No, they've got people for that."

"Do you want me to take tickets?"

"No. I don't know. Let's see what happens."

Brunton basically got paid to hang out for a few months, and then left to start driving a cab and figuring out how to get into the film business.

He designed the handbills, basing them on a template that featured a man (rumoured to be Topp when he was in high school) holding a horseshoe decorated with flowers. He'd alter the face to suit whichever bands were prominent on the flyer.

The handbills were made with Letraset dry transfers, rubber cement, and X-Acto blades. The transfers would be pressed onto the page and then distressed with the knife. If Brunton wanted the colours reversed (that is, black on white rather than white on black), he'd ride his bike up to Midtown Reproductions at Davenport and Yonge, pay ten bucks, and then wait a day to get it back. Brunton had to switch printing houses at least once because of complaints by the owners that he used too much black ink. Once a handbill was completed, hundreds of copies were made

The first poster produced by The Garys (and designed by *The Last Pogo* director Colin Brunton), announcing the beginning of their seminal time booking the Horseshoe Tavern. March 1978.

and then stapled to telephone poles and construction hoardings downtown, careful not to cover up any other current handbills.

Before the gentrification of Queen Street West, the blocks around Spadina were an industrial wasteland of second-hand book and furniture stores. Brunton takes us back to what the Horseshoe neighbourhood looked like then: "Queen Street West was a ghost town of industrial kitchen supply stores, boarded-up storefronts, and used bookstores, edged onto the then still largely Jewish Spadina Avenue, with its delis, milliners, and tailors. There was gravel between the streetcar tracks. On most days, you were lucky to see a handful of people roaming the streets at the corner of Queen and Spadina, where the Horseshoe sat."

Also, Toronto Transit Commission workers went on strike in 1978 for eight days, adding to the ghostly atmosphere. Hitchhiking was common. Cabs, which offered cheap fares, did brisk business along this strip, taking the barflies from club to club.

The Beverley Tavern, the local watering hole for Ontario College of Art students, was just four blocks east and offered an open stage to the new wave bands coming largely from the college. These bands were not interested in playing Rolling Stones covers at some dive bar or restaurant.

Peter Pan restaurant, in business since 1927, was across the street and a block west of the Beverley, and had been given a major do-over by Sandy Stagg two years earlier, in 1976. It was another artist hangout, and many musicians worked there. The seeds of the new Queen Street West scene were planted.

"What Gary [Topp] and I tried to do was take you somewhere you hadn't been before: musically, physically, and spiritually," recalls Cormier. "We were not about serving up the same old thing. We booked a lot of bands that couldn't get the time of day from anywhere else in the city."

Checking out the Horseshoe for the first time, Topp and Cormier were confronted by rounders sitting at the bar slugging back cheap draft beer. A few of these regular barflies asked them bluntly, "You're not going to kick us out, are you?" Cormier assured them they would always be welcome. Even some of the die-hard country fans from the Horseshoe's previous regime, who were surprised by the new and unfamiliar sounds when The Garys took over, were eventually won over by the energy and enthusiasm of the music the promoters brought in. They, too, were ready for a change.

Cormier recalls this cool transformation and musical discovery:

> You saw these people who looked like they had just come in
> from Alberta, real cowboy crowd, and they would be dig-
> gin' the jazz and diggin' the punk stuff; it was bizarre. There
> would be instances when a couple — you knew they weren't
> in the right place — who were dressed up to go downtown,
> had heard about the Horseshoe, came in, and after about
> twenty minutes would come back to the door and tell me,
> "We've been here for a while, this is not really our scene, can
> we get our money back?" and I would give them their money
> back. Then, weeks later I would be at the front door and
> there would be the same couple. I would say "What gives?
> A week ago you said it wasn't your scene," and they said,
> "Everywhere else we've been since is so boring, so here we
> are!" There was a lot of that type of discovery from "the kids."

For The Garys, the scene is what mattered most: art for art's sake. "Gary
and I were never in it for the money," Cormier adds. "We were in it for the
thrills. It was cheaper, more often than not, to bring these bands here, rather
than having to go to New York or Los Angeles or London to see them."

Cormier says a spirit of camaraderie fuelled the scene. People helped
each other.

> The moments I remember most fondly are when an opening
> band, who barely had enough money to get [to] the gig, was
> on stage playing and the guitar player breaks a string; then,
> the roadie for the headlining act runs backstage, gets a guitar,
> brings it back to the player, takes his guitar, brings it back to
> dressing room, restrings it and tunes it up, and brings it back
> to him without nobody missing a beat. It was all so natural.

During those eight months in 1978, the kids in the punk scene would
come out of the Horseshoe — some wearing dog collars — and the cops
would bust them and give them trouble. At the same time, the fanzines,
clothing designers, and independent record stores were all picking up on

the scene and sensing it was seminal; it was all about independence and a do-it-yourself spirit. The punk ethos was about picking up a guitar and putting a band together even if you couldn't play. Kids were experimenting with drugs, and they were experimenting with their instruments, creating new and explosive sounds. While this new music gave some a headache, for those it spoke to, it woke them up to a new reality and altered their lives.

Before The Garys arrived at the Horseshoe, punk was already alive and growing in Toronto, with bands performing at places like the Colonial Underground, the Hotel Isabella, and the Crash 'n' Burn, an old warehouse that was the city's equivalent of New York's infamous CBGB.

Steve Koch moved to Toronto from Calgary specifically because of this underground punk scene. In 1977, he heard the Ramones' *Rocket to Russia*; the sounds, unlike anything he'd ever heard before, spilling from his stereo speakers changed his life. First, he quit university and went to England, figuring if he didn't go then, he would miss the whole movement. After seeing a ton of bands, he returned briefly to Calgary to finish his last semester of university. Then, the first chance he got, he was following the road east with a friend. "I became aware of the Toronto scene via a magazine called *File*," he recalls. "I saw pictures of the Ugly, the Viletones, and the B-Girls and I thought, *I need to be there*, so me and a friend hopped in his car and just starting driving."

The B-Girls.

For Koch, who joined the Viletones after the concert known as The Last Pogo and also played in the Demics, seeing the Dead Boys — a punk band originally hailing from Cleveland, Ohio — was his most memorable 'Shoe show. "It summarized everything about punk rock in my life and in the world," Koch recalls. "If you could distill everything about that whole movement into one little crystal, that was it, that night. It was such an amazing life-affirming thing."

The punk movement mirrored the evolution of Toronto, which at the time was really starting to change culturally, from a staid, conservative, small-town vibe to a city with a sense of chic, combined with an ugly undertone. Though you still couldn't drink on Sundays, speakeasies like the Elephant Walk, across the street from the Horseshoe, started to spring up around town. Further east and north on Yonge Street, music venues like Le Coq d'Or, where Ronnie Hawkins and the Hawks (who became The Band) held court, mixed with strip joints, adult video stores, and other seedy establishments. One stretch of Yonge Street had more massage parlours per capita than anywhere else in North America at the time. "Toronto was starting to get a bit cooler, because before that there really wasn't a thing called the counterculture," says Colin Brunton, who still works in the film and television industry today. "The mainstream press and culture bureaucrats of Toronto still regarded punk as a passing fancy, not worthy of their recognition."

Peter Goddard was one of the few journalists who got it and saw the scene for what it really was — a watershed moment, not merely "a passing fancy." Goddard was brought on to the *Star*'s staff in 1973 as a popular music critic; he covered everything from jazz and big band music to rock 'n' roll, country, and later, the burgeoning punk and new wave scene. Goddard recalls this seminal period:

> What The Garys did was quite spectacular. I remember seeing Cecil Taylor there [at the Horseshoe]. It was a remarkable concert. He was near the end of his career and he played for two hours straight. It was the most muscular music you have ever heard … through-the-roof spectacular. I remember leaving to go write about it and it still seemed out of sync with the Horseshoe. I don't think Gary [Topp], with all the voodoo he is capable of, ever managed to change the vibe of the place. It still felt like a little sleazy country club. He was only booking it.

Topp disagrees with Goddard, insisting he and his partner changed the club's vibe. During those eight months, everybody who came to the Horseshoe was there for a higher purpose. During The Garys' tenure, the club was a destination, not just a live concert venue. Every night was memorable for the unique music and the unique people who attended this short-lived scene. "You have to understand that that club in the eight months we were there was a hangout. It had a completely different atmosphere," Topp says. "It was like a clubhouse for a thousand people who were into building a scene and changing Toronto. Queen Street wasn't like it is now. We weren't just stocking shelves in a grocery store. There weren't as many bands as there are now, but we didn't just book anybody. We had varied offerings; we showed movies, we had comedy … it was a gathering place for a part of the community that was developing a new music scene in Toronto."

That burgeoning punk rock scene in the late 1970s not only grabbed Toronto by the bollocks but also slowly captured the world's attention. Those years changed not just the Horseshoe but also the city and the bourgeoisie, even impacting fashion trends. Picture an eighty-year-old woman walking out of Holt Renfrew in leather pants and to-the-knee matching black boots.

Johnny Thunders and the Heartbreakers on September 8, 1978.

You can attribute that to the punk rock explosion and its trickle-down influence on pop culture. Prior to punk's mainstream appeal, the scene was a tight one, reserved for the Horseshoe Tavern and other like-minded clubs, such as Larry's Hideaway and the Crash 'n' Burn, and their devout followers.

Cleave Anderson, Blue Rodeo's original drummer, recalls driving downtown from Etobicoke in his "summer-of-love blue" Chevrolet Chevelle and parking right in front of one of these taverns. There weren't any cars on the street. Nobody who lived downtown had a car. At the time, he was playing in Battered Wives, a punk band that opened for Elvis Costello across Canada in 1978. The group mostly played Larry's Hideaway and the Crash 'n' Burn, where they had regular lineups around the block. Battered Wives had a rehearsal space right near where the Crash 'n' Burn was, just southeast of the Horseshoe on Nelson Street. It was a warehouse for a second-hand clothing store called Flying Down to Rio, where they would go to pick out their clothes: skinny jeans, satin, velvet, and 1950s jean jackets, which they would dye black and then chop off their collars. While Battered Wives never played the Horseshoe during The Garys' stint booking shows, Anderson and his bandmates would often walk north to Queen Street and check out the show after their rehearsal.

"Most of the people in the beginning in the punk rock scene were artists, suburban ne'er-do-wells," Anderson recalls. "It wasn't the disenfranchised. It was art students who thought rock 'n' roll had lost all its mojo."

Lin Duperron was one of these early devotees to the punk scene. From the moment The Garys took over booking the Horseshoe until the day their tenure ended, she was at the club every day. She was eighteen — just legal to drink — and was in search of a good time. She had moved with her family to the big city when she was a teenager, and she quickly found a home at the 'Shoe. "I felt like I ran the place in some ways, because I was there all the time … it was my turf," she says. Initially, Duperron was drawn to the music. "Our lives push us in different directions. My life led me to that attitude of 'screw everything, I'm going to do my own thing' … being in that scene offered that. There were no rules, no regulations, you wore what you wanted, listened to what you wanted, and stayed up all night. The whole thing was a three-sixty for me, and I needed that at that point in my life."

After a night with little sleep, after crashing on someone's couch, Duperron and her friends — often ten of them — would pile into someone's car, or a cab willing to take them, and spend their days hanging out at

New Rose, a punk rock boutique owned and operated by Margarita Passion. The store was open from Wednesday to Saturday from noon until six. Here, Duperron and her friends played pinball, bought fanzines and 45s and LPs by local bands, or tried on the latest fashions from Margarita. They also met many musicians, who hung out there during the day before their gigs at night. A handbill for the store from that time promised the following: "Sick Stuff for a Sick Society, 4-5's + EP'S by local Anti-Heros [*sic*]."

Besides spending lazy afternoons at New Rose, Duperron and her friends also loitered and drank too much in the front bar at the Horseshoe — playing pinball and pool and whiling away the hours waiting for the sun to set. Eating was an afterthought. At night, they headed to the 'Shoe's back bar to see the latest band The Garys had booked. The next day, the ritual repeated.

*   *   *

On the first Thursday and Friday of November 1978, the Police played a pair of shows at the Horseshoe. Ask around, and thousands claim to have been at one of these concerts. The reality is that, at the most, a few dozen people showed up and paid the four-dollar cover charge to watch a young Sting and his band play a pair of gigs. There was more staff there to watch the Police than paying patrons. Duperron was one of the lucky few who caught the show. She doesn't remember much about it, saying it was "just an ordinary night at the Horseshoe." She still has her ticket stub, though, and a mono test pressing 45 of the single "Roxanne" that she bought that night, proving she was there.

At the time, the Police were not even on tour. The Garys got talking with an agent from England who mentioned the name of these seasoned musicians who had originally formed the year before as a punk band. The Garys were big fans of another cat from across the pond: an eccentric singer-songwriter named Kevin Coyne. Once they learned that Andy Summers, the Police's guitarist, used to play with Coyne, they were intrigued and brought the Police over strictly to play the Horseshoe. The trio, all with their hair dyed blond, consisted of Summers on lead guitar, Stewart Copeland on drums, and Sting on bass and vocals. Before their Horseshoe shows, Cormier took the English musicians to the CHUM-FM radio station. "We were physically escorted out the door," he recalls. "CHUM did not want to know about punk bands."

(Top) The Police pose in the basement dressing room of the Horseshoe; the British band played there in November 1978.
(Bottom) A promotional 45 rpm record of the Police's single "Roxanne," bought by Lin Duperron at the Horseshoe Tavern when the band played there in 1978.

Back at the club, the band played a memorable and tight two-hour set to the small audience, many of whom they got to know by name, and who demanded an encore. As Cormier recalls in the book *Rock and Roll Toronto*, "I walked into the room, and Sting was already undressed. He went back and played in his underwear." The band felt so bad about the poor attendance, they gave The Garys back the two-hundred-dollar fee agreed to in their contract.

Despite this underwhelming turnout and dissing by the media, The Garys proved they were always one step ahead of the musical trends. Six months later, you couldn't turn on a radio anywhere in the world without hearing the Police's hit single "Roxanne" blasting forth; the album featuring the infectious tune would go on to sell two million copies worldwide.

The Garys told the band they could come back to play Toronto any time. The next year the Police would play The Garys' new venue, The Edge. Later, as their stature grew, they hadn't forgotten The Garys giving them that first chance to play in Hogtown, so in 1981 the band headlined a massive concert in Oakville, Ontario, called the Police Picnic that also included the Go-Go's, Iggy Pop, the Specials, Killing Joke, and Canadian acts the Payolas and Nash the Slash. It would be the first of three Police Picnics (the next two were held at Exhibition Place in Toronto), all brought to you by — you guessed it — The Garys.

* * *

The Garys were just starting to make money when manager Peter Graham pulled the plug on the promoters and told them he was changing his booking policies, going back to country and western music. A deal that reportedly was for eight years was cut short after just eight months.

What went wrong, and why the shift? According to Graham, the main issue with The Garys' bookings was the growing clash between Liquor Licensing Board requirements and the realities of a new wave club. As he told the *Globe and Mail* on the eve of this changing of the guard, "People want to walk around and do things during a punk rock concert and they just can't do that in a licensed bar. Just the other day, a big bar had to go before the board because there were sixteen charges laid during a Battered Wives concert."

Another factor in Graham's shifting his policy and ending The Garys' tenure was new legislation he knew would be coming the following January that would allow authorities to close a bar for a week and impose massive fines if any underage drinkers were found. These were risks Graham was not willing to take.

Rather than go quietly into that good night after only eight months (though those who were there say it felt like so much longer), The Garys decided to give their patrons a gift and leave the 'Shoe with a bang with a pair of shows, which they called The Last Pogo and The Last Bound-Up.

The idea behind the names and the concept was taken from The Band's famed farewell concert in 1976 at the Winterland Ballroom in San Francisco, captured beautifully on screen by Martin Scorsese in *The Last Waltz*. Topp recalls, "The night of The Last Bound-Up, Moses Znaimer, Citytv boss, wanted to have a meeting with us, so we met that night before the doors opened. He said, 'I think it's time we bring our cameras in and shoot your shows.' We basically said, 'You are eight months too late!' He didn't have a clue … comes on the last night of our run and says, *I think this music is important*."

That lack of interest from the mainstream media is telling of the time. Only a select few local scribes, like Peter Goddard at the *Toronto Star*, got it, realizing the importance of what The Garys were doing. More often it was the foreign press who got it first. For example, when the pair brought in the popular American new wave band Pere Ubu, the London *Times* and *New Musical Express* each flew two reporters across the pond to cover their Horseshoe appearance. According to Topp, the moniker "The Last Pogo" says it all as far as what was happening at the Horseshoe and what was happening at that pivotal period in Toronto. "The whole scene was us against the wall … us against Toronto," he explains. "There were only about a thousand people, bands included. As it started to pick up, the people who ran the place didn't care and they wanted to go back to booking country music."

Once The Garys were given notice that their services were no longer needed at the Horseshoe, the pair figured, *Well, then, let's go out with a bang*. "We had built up a scene, and it was our goodbye party," Cormier recalls.

The first night, which featured Cormier and Topp's favourite punk bands, including the Viletones and Teenage Head, was called The Last Pogo, and the next night, featuring reggae and new wave groups like Rough Trade, was dubbed The Last Bound-Up. The shows were scheduled for December 1 and 2, 1978.

No handbills or posters were distributed, but those in the scene found out easily enough. The night of The Last Pogo, the place was packed and well over capacity. The walls were sweating.

With an abundance of alcohol flowing — some of the patrons had been drinking all day — by the time the bands started to play, the atmosphere was tense. Record label Bomb Records was there to make a live recording of the two nights, and with rumours that a film was being made as well, The Last Pogo started to become a big deal.

Steven Leckie of the Viletones, who had originally refused to play, crashed the show and did a set with a new lineup. Bass guitarist Sam Ferrara had to borrow a bass from Steve Mahon of Teenage Head and play it upside down because Steve was a leftie. On top of that, Ferrara struggled with a faulty connection, and the audience couldn't even hear the bass. Leckie ended the set by yelling out, "Kill the hippies!" — a directive that the nasty street gang the Blake Street Boys took to heart and acted on a few hours later.

Colin Brunton doesn't recall much of what went on the night of The Last Pogo, but the ending was certainly memorable. "With eight hundred people crammed into the five-hundred capacity bar, draft beer running out and only hard liquor available, and the stench of pot and tobacco smoke

Teenage Head on August 18, 1978.

creating a cloud over the crowd," he explains, "a fat detective drinking at the bar thought that enough was enough. He waddled up to the stage, and told headlining band Teenage Head that the show was over. Bassist Steve Mahon, on a rare night that he'd been drinking, wagged his finger in the cop's face and warned him that there would be trouble if the band didn't get to play. The cop relented and said they could play one song."

Cleave Anderson adds, "It seemed like the first time the place seemed out of control. Up until then, it was mostly a crowd of people you knew. At The Last Pogo, these people come in all of sudden that we didn't know who they were. There was sort of a sense of, *Uh oh, violence.* After The Last Pogo and Sid [Vicious] died — instead of punk being something nobody wanted anything to do with it became a shot in the arm for rock 'n' roll."

After Teenage Head played only a shortened version of their best-known song, "Picture My Face," they walked offstage. The crowd didn't know what was happening, so they went crazy. Topp once compared the sound of this moment of mayhem to "a hundred chainsaws ripping down Algonquin Park." Tables were overturned, chairs and bottles were thrown, and the Blake Street Boys, prompted by Steven Leckie's call to "kill the hippies," beat the crap out of anyone there unlucky enough to have long hair. Swollen Members lead singer Evan Siegel, in a wheelchair as his persona Dr. Strangelove, never broke character and wheeled his way to safety. Brunton and his crew were literally kicked to the curb, where they joined hundreds of others out on the street. Yellow cop cars pulled up and forced the boisterous crowd to disperse. Somehow sound recordist Dave Gebe managed to stay inside and capture the sound of the destruction. Brunton, Lee, and the two camera operators managed to sneak back inside and get images of the devastation, stopping only when a heartbroken Horseshoe regular from before The Garys' time pleaded with them to stop.

"It was more than just a party gone awry," recalls Lin Duperron, "it was mayhem." Duperron knew everybody from the punk crowd, but she admits she also knew the Blake Street Boys through a friend, Ally, who lived around the corner from her mom's house. The pair used to hang out. "Some of his friends were a little sketchy and a little nuts, especially when they were drinking," she recalls.

Duperron and her friends had been at the Horseshoe partying and drinking all day. Everybody was getting really "sloshed," she says, and then

The Viletones on September 2, 1978.

the Viletones went on. "People were drunk, bouncing into each other, throwing each other around, and things started to get a little bit aggressive," she remembers. "All of a sudden from the stage Steven Leckie yells, 'Let's kill the hippies!' Suddenly, the Blake Street Boys jump my friend.... I turn around and see my friend getting the shit kicked out of him while the band is still playing." She continues:

> The band's bassist, Sam [Ferrara], had his head down and is oblivious to what is going on. I reach to his bass strings and [pull] on them and said, "Shut the fuck up!" No one knew what was happening in front of the stage. It was packed. My friend is on the ground, and they are putting the boots to his face. I started blocking his face — kicking their feet — I had bruises from my ankles to my thighs from blocking their shots. He had shoe imprints on his forehead ... it was nasty. All hell was breaking loose. The band finally stopped and then you heard things being broken.

Concertgoers and police outside the Horseshoe Tavern following The Last Pogo, when the final show under The Garys' reign came to an unfortunate conclusion with the cops shutting down the bar; arrests and a small riot ensued. December 2, 1978.

I remember Motor coming out saying we needed to get the hell out of there. A few friends grabbed Nathan and took him out the back. I came back and remember seeing someone doing the crab on the ground, walking backwards trying to escape as someone is breaking a chair over top of him. Johnny Garbagecan had his jaw broken. The violence was so intense. People had no idea how much they were hurting each other. That's how it ended.

Cop cars lined the street outside from Spadina to Peter. Police officers took turns rounding up concertgoers as they piled out of the club — not the type of press The Garys were hoping for from The Last Pogo.

Reflecting back on that night, Duperron can't explain what happened, why people got so violent. Perhaps putting a label on it — "The Last" — may have escalated things. Combine that with copious amounts of alcohol and a venue that was well over capacity, and anyone can see it was a recipe for disaster.

When The Garys' reign came to an abrupt stop following The Last Pogo and the ensuing riot, and The Last Bound-Up, it marked the end of an era.

For Duperron, it was a sad time. "We were all family," she says. "When the club closed down, it was like a bunch of lost puppies not sure where we would go from there."

As Gary Cormier told the *Globe and Mail* back in 1978, twenty-four hours before their final show, he didn't see their eight-month run as a failure. Far from it. "We accomplished everything we intended to do." The pair never took the tried and true road — always preferring the paths less travelled. Of that, Cormier is proud. "Whenever we've tried to play it safe rather than just following our own instincts, we've blown it," he told the *Globe*.

As far as Topp is concerned, that brief moment in time changed not just the Horseshoe but also Toronto. "Everybody knew each other," he says. "It was a smaller industry, but it was an up-and-coming industry. We were fortunate to be aware of, and like, the groundbreaking artists of that time." He adds, "It's a time that can't be recaptured. It was like life and death for the people in the scene and for us, too, because we were the ones putting our money into it for the things we loved."

The Garys would be out of action for only a couple of months, eventually opening The Edge at Church and Gerrard, where they would continue the against-the-grain booking policy they had started at the Horseshoe, eventually winning a Toronto Arts Award for their efforts.

5

The Show Hank Williams Never Gave

Willing suspension of disbelief ...
— Samuel Taylor Coleridge

HANK WILLIAMS IS AS LEGENDARY a figure in the annals of country
music as the Horseshoe is in Toronto's music history. In his short time on this
earth — just twenty-nine years — Williams issued only thirty singles, but
eleven of them went to number one. These hits were recorded over less than six
years, between December 1946 and September 1952. It's a surprise, then, to
learn that Hank, who released his first hit single, "Move It On Over," the same
year Jack Starr opened his club, never played the Queen Street institution.

In fact, in his short career Williams played Toronto only a couple of
times: once in 1949 at the Mutual Street Arena, and later at Maple Leaf
Gardens. Hank Williams died in the back of his Cadillac sometime in the
early morning on New Year's Day 1953.

There are rumours, however, that the honky-tonker, known for such
classics as "Hey Good Lookin'," "Cold, Cold Heart," and "Jambalaya," did
visit the Toronto tavern.

Former manager and talent booker X-Ray MacRae shares a conversation
he had one day with Leon Redbone, a champion of early American ragtime,
blues, and jazz, who was at the bar for an interview:

> I walked in one day, and Leon Redbone and MuchMusic
> host Denise Donlon were standing by the pool table in the
> front bar. Leon was a pool shark, and she [Donlon] wanted

to do the interview at the Horseshoe because they had a pool table. Eventually, he drifted away from Denise and asked me, "Can we go down to your office?"

I said, "Why?" And he replied, "I'll tell you after." My office was down in the back corner near the old draft refrigerator in the basement. We get in there and he said, "I'm honoured to be here." I said, "Why is that?"

"Because," he said, "I grew up in Buffalo, and Hank Williams was one of my heroes when I was young. I heard a story that Hank hid out in the office of the Horseshoe for three days pilled and drugged out and Jack Starr put him up in the office."

While it's uncertain whether the real Hank ever set foot in the Horseshoe, for a brief period in 1979 and 1980, more than twenty-five years after Hank's tragic death, many 'Shoe patrons attended the stage play *Hank Williams: The Show He Never Gave*, which was performed by Sneezy Waters.

Part tribute, part musical tragedy, the performance was so real many thought Hank had risen from the dead. Richard Flohil, a long-time Toronto concert promoter and music man about town who marketed the Hank Williams shows back in the late 1970s, recalls a funny moment from that time: "The first day, Sneezy went downstairs for a pee and there was this bottle-blond woman who thought he was Hank. She grabs him and says, 'I saw you in Belleville.' Sneezy was totally freaked out. That was why we had a car waiting for him; the moment he got off stage, he was to get right into the car. While they were still yelling for an encore, he was already back at the Westbury Hotel at Yonge and College where we put up the band."

Today, Sneezy Waters (né Peter Hodgson) lives in Ottawa. He changed his name in 1972 for no reason other than he liked the ring of it and hoped it might help his budding music career. At seventy, he's working as a union stagehand at the National Arts Centre but he still plays gigs here and there. Like the character of Hank he inhabited for many years, Waters has fought a lot of his own demons. Unlike Hank, however, he's been successful. He quit drinking at forty-three. He doesn't even smoke dope anymore. "I've got so much more energy, and it is all real!" he says. At the time, though, battling those demons certainly helped him transform himself into the troubled Williams.

Before he took on the role of Hank in Maynard Collins's play *Hank Williams: The Show He Never Gave*, Sneezy was a gigging musician who had

Sneezy Waters (né Peter Hodgson) stars in the Maynard Collins's play *Hank Williams: The Show He Never Gave* at the Horseshoe in December 1978.

already played the Horseshoe a couple of times. He recalls a small stage that was on the side, in the middle of the room, at the end of the bar. "You were right on top of each other, and the ceiling was so low."

Looking back today, the singer and guitar-picker speculates that the fact that he had played there previously is what opened the door for booking him when it came time to bring the Hank Williams show to Toronto. Really, what better place could there have been to host a show about one of the legendary outlaws and early pioneers of country music than the Horseshoe Tavern?

So how did Sneezy — who didn't have any acting experience — land the role of Williams in the play? Flash back to the late 1970s: Waters was busking for coins in Ottawa's ByWard Market late one afternoon when his old friend Maynard Collins came by, handed him a script, and asked him to read it. "It's about the last night of a country singer's life," Collins told him.

Collins figured Sneezy could learn to act because, more important, he already had half of what was needed to pull off the feat — he had been listening to, learning, and performing some of Hank's songs in his sets for years. It also helped that he could yodel, one of the trademarks of Hank's unique vocal delivery. This chance encounter led to a successful long-term partnership between the pair, and the script would become the basis of a play that was performed across Canada to sold-out audiences at least eight hundred times over the ensuing decades. It also became a feature film that screened at the Toronto International Film Festival, but because the music rights couldn't be secured for a theatrical release, the movie aired only on television in Canada.

Waters recalls his musical upbringing and how it played a part in his landing this role:

> My brother and I had grown up on that old-time country stuff. The only records we had were a box of 45s, equivalent of one LP — six singles came in one box. This included songs like "I've Just Told Mama Goodbye," "Six More Miles to the Graveyard," all these lugubrious tunes. Hank's classic "Lovesick Blues" was also on there. We used to sing all these songs while growing up even before we learned to play an instrument.

The play premiered in the nation's capital at the Beacon Arms in 1977, and the next year Sneezy and the playwright and producer, Maynard Collins, took the show on the road, heading to Toronto for a ten-day string of dates in early December 1978.

The previous year during the The Garys' stint at the 'Shoe, they had booked in movies and some other acts that blurred the boundaries among theatre, music, vaudeville, and burlesque, but *Hank Williams: The Show He Never Gave* was one of the first times a play had been performed at the Horseshoe Tavern. Following on the heels of a year that had culminated in The Last Pogo and The Last Bound-Up, it certainly was a one-eighty-degree shift in programming.

A poster advertising *Hank Williams: The Show He Never Gave*, which premiered at the Beacon Arms Hotel in Ottawa before moving on to the Horseshoe Tavern; later, it was made into a feature film.

The show appealed to the patrons from the bar's country and western heyday as well as a wide assortment of folks who had read the rave reviews in the *Ottawa Citizen* and had heard the buzz before the play was even booked. One country music reviewer, writing for the *Citizen*, wrote a piece as if Hank Williams was actually playing in town. At the end of the review, just to make sure readers weren't completely fooled, the reporter wrote, "Hank Williams was the greatest country singer and Sneezy Waters is him. If Hank is dead, who is this?"

"That set us up to go down to Toronto," Sneezy recalls.

Sneezy tried his best to be faithful to the music and to Hank's revered status in the music world — how he had burned out at twenty-nine, the songs he threw away, how he performed them, and how he was so well loved even in his darkest moments. Judging by the reviews from the day, he more than succeeded.

The whole concept behind *Hank Williams: The Show He Never Gave* is imagining what it would have been like if Hank had come back for one more show on New Year's Day 1952 (he'd died the previous night in the back seat of a car while driving to a show in Canton, Ohio). Hank's ghost offers the audience barroom hallucinations and dreams that he was playing for a room full of people as he lay dying. The show transports the audience back to an era when country and western music, like Hank's heartfelt catalogue, grabbed radio listeners and sold records. Songs such as "Your Cheatin' Heart," "Hey Good Lookin'," and the first-ever tears-in-your-beer song "I'm So Lonesome I Could Cry."

At the Horseshoe, Sneezy and his band dressed in period costumes similar to those that Hank and his band would have worn. Sneezy wore replicas of Hank's cowboy boots and dressed in a suit with music notes down the sleeves. The band also sported haircuts from that era and used period guitars, on which they duplicated the old-fashioned country licks for which Williams and his band were famous. The Horseshoe Tavern was transformed, too, taking on the atmosphere and ambience of a country and western saloon circa 1952. "They moved everything out of there, like the TVs, that were later than the date that Hank died," recalls the show's promoter, Richard Flohil. "To make it more realistic, they hung banners that said 'Happy New Year!'"

For Flohil, the best part of the play, what made it even more realistic, was Hank's monologue between songs, in which, in an alcohol-and-drug-induced haze, he rambled on about the meaning of life, death, love, politics, hate, and heaven and hell. He would say stuff like "I hope our boys come back from Korea safely!" and "That young Nixon is going to be good."

Hank Williams: The Show He Never Gave certainly blurred the lines between theatre and real life. Some drunken patrons, a little delusional, too, after watching Sneezy's convincing performance, would try to get on stage to talk to Hank. They didn't believe he was an actor. At times Sneezy, too, believed he was Hank. As he told the *Toronto Star* in an interview in 1978, "Sometimes, I think I *am* Hank Williams up there. I get buzzes into the man himself. Usually when I hit that perfect note, just like Hank hits it on the record, or I feel I've pulled off one of my lines with just the right emotion and I can sense the impact on the audience."

Frequently, Sneezy left people — both women and men — in tears. After one particular show, country singer and actor Jerry Reed came out of the audience, tears in his eyes, and embraced Sneezy, saying in a choked-up voice, "Beautiful, man, just beautiful."

The play began with the boys hanging out in the dressing room. Then, they climbed up from the basement and sauntered right onto the stage, waiting for Hank, who stumbled out after a while, clearly already a few sheets to the wind.

At the end of the show, Hank made his exit, and there was never a curtain call. Instead, Hank (a.k.a. Sneezy) would stumble off stage following a long and meandering religious spiel while the band played "I Saw the Light." There would always be a huge standing ovation, everyone thumping on the tables and yelling for an encore.

Sneezy has this to say about this theatre trick: "When he was gone, he had to be gone. The idea was that Hank was leaving to die, so what's the point of him coming back? This made people even more wistful and quizzical about it … they couldn't quite figure it out. That's as close as I ever got to what the big stars must go through. I came off the stage, went downstairs, grabbed my parka, and then headed outside and grabbed a cab in the alley at the Horseshoe, and away I would go."

Of all the shows he performed as Hank at the Horseshoe, a couple stand out for Sneezy. One night, because of the low ceiling and how the lights are right above you, it was pretty warm. He was wearing a suit and hat, and had his tie done up tight just like Hank: "I'm doing my line and I'm not supposed to respond to anyone in the audience when this old guy comes right up to me at the stage, it was just a foot riser, weaving his way through all the chairs and tables of people drinking beers, and he holds out his hand. I wasn't looking at him. I was trying to look everywhere else. Finally, I look and he is handing me a tissue. I thanked him, wiped my sweaty brow, and then carried on."

Another time, George, the pedal steel player, was facing the audience and there was a woman in the front row; she was one of those people who would sing along with every song even when they don't know the words. Sometimes she would sing two seconds behind Sneezy, and it was really getting to the musician. He was really into Hank's character at that point in the show, in a low, moody place, so he turned to her and, in his best Williams imitation, said, "Honey, I can't even think while you're doing that!" She responded, "Sorry, Hank!"

Playing the part of Hank Williams night in and night out was exhausting. Waters had to be totally in character twenty-four hours a day. He watched what he smoked and drank — and even took up jogging because he wanted his voice to be as strong as possible to mimic the country star's yodel. To prepare for the role, he also watched old tapes of Hank performing, listened to radio broadcasts from the early 1950s, and studied old black-and-white photographs. He even got tips from some of Hank's contemporaries. Minnie Pearl, who played the Grand Ole Opry for nearly fifty years before her death in 1996, was one of these old-time Nashville legends who helped Sneezy transform into Hank. Pearl's husband was a pilot and would have flown Hank up to Canton, Ohio, on that fateful night if the weather had been good. Pearl gave Sneezy a few tips, such as how to walk like Hank and how he held his head and stood at the microphone, with his legs slightly bent.

Waters had this to say about meeting the country comedian:

> One day, we went to Cornwall where Minnie was touring as part of an Opry-packaged show. Collins showed her a picture of me in a Cadillac, and she said, "Where did you get this?" I told her to understand that we were giving Hank as much dignity as possible. Minnie replied that the last time she saw Hank he had as much dignity as a wounded dog, so it would be very hard for us to overdo the pathos that marked the end of his life. The last time she saw him was in Oklahoma City where she found him in the well of a desk crying.

Director Peter Froehlich was another key to the play's successful run, Sneezy says. This wonderful, experimental theatre guy calmed him down, worked "the snot out of him," and taught him a few tricks of the trade along the way. "He picked up on a lot of things that I don't think another director would have seen. One afternoon, we were rehearsing and I had this thing where Hank is kind of pissed, but he is trying to ingratiate himself with the audience. Hank loved baseball and comic books, so I asked, 'Are there any baseball fans out there?' Well, before they could answer, I said, 'I love the Brooklyn Dodgers, but the Yankees beat them again this year; maybe next year will be their turn.' Then, I introduced the song 'You Win Again,' dedicating it to all those losers out there."

Sneezy had all of Hank's mannerisms down: from his noncommittal stare to tuning out the audience when it played into his favour. He says he owed all of that to Froehlich, who rewrote some of the script and words to match Hank's reactions to certain situations, such as when people would yell, "Sing it again, Hank!" or "Have another one!" in reference to his penchant for the drink. Waters just ignored them and tactfully accepted their applause with a sombre smile and a faraway look in his eyes.

Despite later taking *Hank Williams: The Show He Never Gave* across Canada and to a few select shows south of the border, more than thirty-five years on the Horseshoe Tavern shows remain some of Sneezy's most memorable performances: "One time, years later, when I was at the front bar, the caretaker of the building came up to me, and in broken English, tugged at my sleeve, and said, 'You know your son played here one time?' I was like, 'I don't have any kids. What are you talking about?' Finally, it dawned on me that he was talking about Hank Williams Jr. He was totally convinced I was Hank Williams. Those are sweet things that happened in my life."

6

The 'Shoe Rises Again

Fall seven times, stand up eight.
— Japanese proverb

ON A SAD SATURDAY in December 1982 — one year shy of the Horseshoe Tavern's thirty-fifth birthday — the name on the marquee, synonymous with Queen Street West for more than three decades, came down. As the lights flickered out, the Horseshoe Tavern, at least in name, shut its doors. The storied tavern Jack Starr had built seemed it would be no more. Thankfully, this was only temporary.

Unlike the musical mayhem and melee that had ended The Garys' era, this finale was more subdued; the sombre event billed as The Last Day of Country Music paid homage to the genre Starr had first brought to the Horseshoe stage back in the 1950s. Memorabilia like posters and framed autographed photographs of all the Grand Ole Opry stars who had played there in those decades — a defining era in the 'Shoe's history — were auctioned off to the highest bidder. Apparently, even the letters of the iconic Horseshoe street sign were sold. Some say a corrupt accountant who worked for one of the local radio stations bought many of these items. Neither the man nor many of these artifacts were ever seen again.

Regardless, the true history of the building — as this book shows, and the interviews with the artists attest — is not found in black-and-white photographs of yesterday's stars. Nor is it found in faded signs and signifiers of a time long past. The Horseshoe has always had a knack for reinventing itself and adapting to the times. Like they say, history has a history of repeating. And it wouldn't be long before this iconic Toronto musical institution was resurrected, guided by a new business model and new owners who shared Starr's original vision and passion. The spirits trapped in the walls of 370 Queen Street West would rise again.

Before this rise from the ruins, the 'Shoe's front room was divided into three spaces, two of which became retail stores: one for men's clothing, and the other for antiques. Then, a new bar — a 1950s club called Stagger Lee's — was opened at the back. Most likely, the name referenced the popular American folk song about the murder of Billy Lyons by "Stag" Lee Shelton in St. Louis, Missouri, in 1895. A version of this tune by Lloyd Price reached number one on the *Billboard* Hot 100 in 1959.

This period is a footnote in the Horseshoe's hallowed history few care to remember. Instead of live music belching from amplifiers, fifties rock 'n' roll music rained from the overhead speakers hung in the rafters. Tables were covered in checkered tablecloths, and waiters with slicked-back hair took patrons' orders. Randy Lanctot was the face behind this transformation, one which was unwelcome to the 'Shoe's dedicated and loyal patrons, who considered the removal of the name a slap in the face. Lanctot understood this weight he carried by betraying the bar's legacy. As the restaurateur joked to Liam Lacey of the *Globe and Mail* a couple of days before Stagger Lee's grand opening, "I keep having this picture in my head that somebody's going to walk in here on Saturday with a gun and take a shot at me."

Even before Lanctot assumed the bar's lease following The Garys' eight-month run in 1978, a couple of managers — whose names are now long since forgotten — had tried unsuccessfully to bring back the country music formula that had initially made the 'Shoe famous.

As musician Andrew Cash (of L'Étranger, Ursula, and the Cash Brothers) explains, when Lanctot arrived in the early 1980s, there wasn't much of a music industry in town. Yet, people still played live for the love of the performance. "When I reflect back on that time, there was no real thought about who was going to make it or what making it was, just about whether you were going to play a good show," he recalls.

Lanctot had taken over the leasing and day-to-day management of the Horseshoe shortly after The Garys' tenure ended, though Starr still owned the building. First, he tried to return to the tavern's roots, but the country music formula of the past did not prove successful, with the new clientele being more interested in cover bands than original music performed by local musicians. Toronto just didn't warrant a country club anymore. Most of the older patrons who truly cared to stomp and line dance to the latest Nashville sounds had since married and moved farther from the downtown core, or even out west to places like Calgary.

Having run a similar club in Ottawa (Arnold's), Lanctot certainly hoped his new venture would succeed; he partnered with Sandy Graham, who ran a 1950s nostalgia spot in Toronto called Route 66, in the hopes of making the Horseshoe Tavern profitable again. "I've got to do what I know best," he told the *Globe and Mail*. "I've sunk something like $100,000 in this place. We're talking my Ottawa club, my home and my possessions. If this doesn't work, it's personal bankruptcy for me."

Flash forward to the spring of 1983: Stagger Lee's 1950s club is not making money. Rumours (perhaps best forgotten) persist to this day that the bar even became a strip club for a few months. While no one ended up taking a shot at the new owner, bankruptcy did rear its ugly head and Lanctot was out, returning to Ottawa to run Barrymore's Music Hall. With interest rates soaring to a staggering 22 percent, it's not surprising the club management business in the early 1980s was a challenge. Today, if you look up by the back bar, near the stage, you'll see a life-size movie poster for the 1963 musical comedy *Bye Bye Birdie*, starring Dick Van Dyke and Ann-Margret, still plastered to the ceiling — the only reminder that Stagger Lee's was ever there.

Marcus O'Hara (brother of actress Catherine O'Hara) and a few others did stints as bar owners that were as short as TV sports timeouts. Each tried to revive the Horseshoe, but all attempts proved to be just as futile as Lanctot's. With little business sense, some of these owners even hosted horseshoe tournaments in the back alley, focusing little on bar sales or bringing in top-tier talent. The venue was bleeding money fast; what was once a solid real estate investment for the Starr family was now a liability.

"They were operating it as a joke," says Kenny Sprackman, who would soon take over, bringing with him a groundbreaking new business model. The story goes that O'Hara sold his interest in the Horseshoe for a lifetime of free drinks at the bar.

Sprackman, it turned out, was just what the place needed.

* * *

The time had come for the Horseshoe Tavern's founder and building owner, Jack Starr, to come out of retirement and look to find a new manager to revive his beloved tavern and make it a mecca for live music again. At the time, Art Clairman, Starr's son-in-law, was managing the building's lease on Starr's behalf.

Kenny Sprackman had recently revived the Hotel Isabella, located just off Yonge Street. Thanks to a tip from his father, who was then working as a bankruptcy trustee, Sprackman had learned about the failing nightclub and, using his hard-nosed business sense and on-the-ground DIY publicity, saved the Isabella from receivership. Within a year, the venue was a major force in the emerging punk, rockabilly, and new wave music scenes. It was there that bands like the Parachute Club played (before they were known as the "Parachute Club" and their top forty hit "Rise Up" skyrocketed up the charts).

After a couple of years at "the Izzy," Sprackman, too, could not compete with the high-flying interest rates and lost the hotel to the banks in 1982. Following a couple more adventures in various bars, the free-spirited Sprackman decided to take a hiatus from the club management business; instead, the entrepreneur picked up some odd jobs here and there while figuring out what venture to try next.

One of these temporary gigs was driving cars south from Toronto to Florida for Canadian snowbirds. Art Clairman's parents were two of these recent retirees; they had owned Claires Cigar Store on Bayview Avenue. By chance, in the fall of 1983, Sprackman ended up driving the Clairmans' car down to the Sunshine State. He did the same thing the following spring. The Clairmans were pleased with Sprackman's work. The message filtered its way back to Art, and through these conversations it wasn't long before word of this young man and his successful background of managing clubs found its way back to Jack. This fortuitous meeting between Art Clairman and Kenny Sprackman led to a formal meeting between Jack and Kenny. During a long lunch at the Simpson Tower, the two men sealed a deal in which Kenny would join a pair of others Starr had recently recruited — Richard Kruk and Michael "X-Ray" MacRae — to manage the day-to-day operations of the Horseshoe and book bands.

Gary Clairman recounts how this transpired:

> My dad is no businessman, but he would give anyone a chance. Kenny always delivered the car on time and carried my grandparents' bags right into the house. The fact he

was Jewish also meant something. My dad sat down with Kenny and gave him the deal of a lifetime. He told him, "Kenny, as you succeed, I'll succeed." He gave Kenny a chance ... Kenny took the ball and ran with it.

During the time when O'Hara was managing the place, the Starrs had already recruited Kruk and MacRae. Not long after, O'Hara was happy to step aside, and, as previously mentioned, he left the business in exchange for a lifetime of free drinks at the bar. And so Sprackman inherited two partners whom he had never met. He later described this partnership to the *Toronto Star*'s Rosie DiManno:

> The Starrs thought, here's a perfect marriage. But I didn't know these guys; we didn't run in the same circles. And at first they were suspicious. After all, they had already been running the 'Shoe with the Starrs. No, their partner says, I'm selling out to this guy. But we felt each other out and discovered, hey, we really like each other. We got along well from the beginning. Here's X-Ray, he's the salt of the earth. And Richard, he's the creative end, the one with all the great ideas. And together the three of us are all after the same thing. We're hardworking, hard-driving, fun-loving individuals.

Sprackman admits that even though the three had their differences, they were always a team. That's one of the main reasons the Horseshoe Tavern continues to exist today. As Richard Kruk says, "Our natures are very different, our experiences are different, and we have strong individual characters. But we teamed up as professionals and we educated each other in the process."

In short order, plans were formulated to usher in a new Horseshoe Tavern era and to revive the bar's "legendary" status. Sprackman, who describes himself in that same *Star* article as "a bottom-line guy," was the ringleader of this motley crew. Later, the three partners adopted the moniker X-L Boys, due to their size. In transforming the 'Shoe, Sprackman relied on the discipline, business principles, and training in numbers he had learned from his father. (Kenny had briefly worked for his dad years earlier in his accounting firm.) By the time he took over managing the Horseshoe, he had also already owned both a Mr. Sub sandwich shop and a Howard Johnson's franchise, run an automobile dealership, and sold real estate. With his varied business knowledge and background, it turned out Sprackman was exactly the guy the Horseshoe needed to right the ship.

The first step was to invest in the deteriorating interior. The new managers renovated and restored the 'Shoe's footprint. The previous owners had boarded up the bar in the back half of the backroom, where Stagger Lee's had briefly lived, so that was one of the first jobs. Second, the stage was moved — returning it to the rear of the backroom where it remains to this day. The club was also split into two distinct areas: a long, narrow bar in the front and a larger bar for live music in the back — giving the renovated space a neighbourhood vibe, inviting to a variety of folks. If you wanted to just come in and have a drink, the front bar was the place. If music was your thing, you could wander to the back, pay the cover, and get ready to rock.

Next, Sprackman, who shared the same entrepreneurial spirit and energetic personality as Starr, tapped into his industry contacts — bringing in Rick Boffo and Brock Adamson to handle the sound. Using the same formula of success he had relied upon in his Hotel Isabella days, Sprackman started bringing in new, rising talent and established bands, booking the musicians by the week or for three- and four-night stands. Derek Andrews was also brought in to help X-Ray find and book talent. Within four months, the debt that had been crippling the joint had been retired. With a knack for seeing the trends before they occurred, Sprackman brought the bookings in line with the current tastes of the current twenty-somethings. Suddenly, there was a ton of money in the bank and the fate of the bar had been turned around. Sprackman says he used a chunk of that money as a down payment to buy an ownership share in the Horseshoe, which he added to over the years; he still owns a small stake today. The philosophy was to bring back the friendly vibe started by Starr. Sprackman always described the atmosphere he tried to create in his establishments, especially the Horseshoe Tavern, as one that was inviting. To him, the 'Shoe was always like a second home. As he once told the *Star*, "We offer an atmosphere that's relaxed and easygoing, with no pretension, no glitz. You come into my place, it's like coming into my house, coming into my living room."

It was the Sprackman (along with X-Ray and Kruk) era that brought back respectability to the Horseshoe Tavern and rejuvenated the old dame. The family-like atmosphere returned, along with the spirit that had fuelled it since

1947, thanks to managers and bookers who were passionate music lovers and also possessed an acute business sense — the same recipe that made the bar such a success during Starr's years at the helm. Sprackman was quoted in the *Globe and Mail* before the bar's fortieth anniversary: "When we took over Jack Starr sent us a three-page typed letter explaining his secrets for success at the Horseshoe. As it happened, it was more or less how we wanted to run the club."

Looking back, it's one of the finest periods in the venue's illustrious history. Today, as a silent partner, Sprackman still maintains a small share in the business; he's now owned a piece of the tavern for as long as Jack Starr did.

*   *   *

During his time at the Hotel Isabella, Kenny Sprackman learned a lot from rock impresario Joe Fried. The pair came up with a new way to pay bands, which, once Sprackman perfected it at the 'Shoe, became the industry standard. In simplistic terms, the new model involved door splits. Until the 1980s, the standard way bar bands were paid was based on flat union rates. "He's the one, along with me, that's an unsung hero of the Canadian music industry," says Sprackman. "We kicked the union reps and agents out of the Isabella and dealt directly with the bands; we made them partners."

Until then, the model for paying musicians in the clubs was as follows: the band might get $1,500, but by the time the agent took their 25 percent and the union siphoned off their dues, artists were working for a pittance. According to Sprackman, there's never a reason for a union to be collecting dues from "garage bands" in clubs.

What Sprackman and Fried also did was help the bands with promotion. The duo plastered posters all around the downtown core, similar to the tactic The Garys patented back in 1978. "We went out every day," Sprackman recalls. "We had no money to advertise."

Sprackman approached the bands with his new proposition, explaining the simple formula: *Forget dealing with an agent; forget giving the union a cut. Instead, you deal directly with us.* He told them they would poster and promote their shows if the artists pitched in and helped spread the word about their gigs to family, fans, and friends. For this partnership, he offered them 50 percent of the door and 25 percent of bar sales. Eventually musicians bought into this new model, realizing that the upside and potential financial returns far outweighed any downsides. This new payment model also led to club owners having a hand in developing the talent and taking a more active role in seeking out bands to book, rather than waiting for an artist's agent to come begging to them to showcase one of the bands on their roster. Once Sprackman took over at the Horseshoe, he implemented this formula, which eventually evolved into one that today is a worldwide standard in clubland: owners keep the bar sales, and the artists keep the proceeds from the door. "That turned out to be a good deal for the bands," says Andrew Cash. "It was really important for bands like us back in those early days."

In Starr's era, artists often played full weeks. X-Ray and Sprackman also created a new booking system that featured local or national touring acts on the weekends — usually one band from Thursday to Saturday, playing three sets a night — mixing in monthly mid-week residencies and American or European touring acts early in the week. The Horseshoe eventually became a preferred showcase for local promoters Concert Productions International (CPI), who were almost assured that the 'Shoe's built-in audience — accentuated by the music industry types and celebrities drinking in the newly created front bar — would accelerate an artist's career development.

Sprackman also made some minor moves with the hired help. A few staff were let go, and he brought in bartender Bob Maynard, who had worked for him at the Isabella, as a barkeep in the front room. Later, he hired Teddy Fury, a drummer without previous bartending experience but with the personality needed to tend bar in the back. The pair still hold court behind the tavern's two bars today. (More to come on these two guys later.)

By 1995, Sprackman knew the times were a changin' yet again, and the bar needed some fresh, young blood to head up the booking and talent buying. That's when he wooed current majority owner Jeff Cohen and his partner, Craig Laskey. "They were our competition," Sprackman recalls. "They were wiping our ass! As the saying goes, 'Keep your enemies close.' That's what I did, and that's how we kept the 'Shoe going. You've got to change with the times. I had the foresight and the gumption when things started to get slow. I knew I needed to change the talent buyer."

As Sprackman explains it, you keep getting older but your audience usually is getting younger. The patrons whom you once booked bands for now have kids and mortgages, and many are living in the suburbs; they are no longer coming out to support bands, seeing live music, or sitting in a bar five nights a week. It's a whole different atmosphere. For a music venue to survive, you need to change with the times. "We needed to start bringing in bands that would bring in the youth," adds Sprackman.

This transition started when Yvonne Matsell took over booking from X-Ray in the early 1990s, discovering bands like the Barenaked Ladies and the Lowest of the Low. And then that's exactly what Cohen and Laskey did, starting in 1995, by bringing over the types of bands they had been show-casing north on Spadina at the El Mocambo.

In recent years, Sprackman fought and successfully beat cancer. He even survived a lightning strike that hit a tree two inches away from him. Now in his mid-sixties, he rarely makes it to downtown Toronto anymore or to the Queen Street bar that was once his home away from home. "I've owned eight or ten other venues in my lifetime, but none of them have the feel of the Horseshoe," he says. "It's like an old pair of slippers."

Still, that old vibe, which once existed for Sprackman every time he strolled in to 370 Queen Street West, is now gone. "When I walk in there now, I don't feel a part of it," he says. "I was there for seven days and seven nights for oh so many years. My clothing. My life. It was the Horseshoe. For a long time, it was my living room and all the people there were my guests. But, it's not my life anymore. I've left that all behind."

*   *   *

X-Ray MacRae recounts how he got recruited into the Horseshoe's herd by his former business partner: "I was sitting at home in Kingston and I heard this old car pull up, and it was Richard Kruk and [Dan] Aykroyd. Kruk said, 'We are going to New York City to open the Hard Rock Cafe on Fifty-Seventh Avenue, and I want you to come and be my partner in the Horseshoe Tavern in Toronto. Here are the keys; see you later."

His friend Richard Kruk had left Kingston for Toronto, where he owned and operated Crooks on Front Street and was looking to expand his real estate footprint in Ontario's capital. X-Ray was unemployed at the time and contemplating driving his motorcycle on an adventure. With nothing to lose, he rolled the dice and took his friend up on his offer.

On April Fool's Day, 1984, X-Ray arrived in Toronto with only two hundred dollars in his pocket along with the keys to the Horseshoe. For the first six months, he slept on a friend's floor. X-Ray had experience in the bar business: he'd worked for eight years as a bartender in Kingston at Dollar Bills, another infamous but short-lived establishment, and later at the Prince George, a century-old Kingston institution that booked rock 'n' roll acts. So he had gotten to know the music scene and some of its players. Later, he owned a record store called Used Grooves. That's where he'd first met actor Dan Aykroyd, and the pair became fast friends over a shared passion for vinyl.

Once in a while, X-Ray would shut his store for a day and he and a friend would make the trek west on the King's Highway to Toronto to check out the bands playing at the Horseshoe, like Platinum Blonde. "It was completely different back in those days," MacRae recalls. "The bar was all blocked and built in. We quickly tore that down, tore down the ceiling, and put up some posters, like [of] The Who's original album." Besides plastering the walls with posters, they also lined the wall behind the back bar from floor to ceiling with old LP records featuring titles by the likes of Lefty Frizzell, Lloyd Price, and Red Foley.

X-Ray dispels one of the many myths about the Horseshoe: Aykroyd was never a part of the bar in an official capacity. Many people think he was some sort of silent partner, but he never was, according to X-Ray. "He was just a friend and a champion of the tavern. I knew him from Kingston. I owned a used record store, and he used to come in and spin discs until the wee hours of the morning. That's when he was doing the *Blues Brothers* thing and was always looking for tunes."

As the Horseshoe business boomed, Kruk, Sprackman, and X-Ray opened up a third establishment (in addition to Crooks), a restaurant called X-Rays, east of the 'Shoe on Queen Street West; later, they opened the Ultrasound Showbar, a new music venue, above the restaurant.

Around 1987, the trio swapped shares, so Kruk took over the management of Ultrasound, Crooks, and X-Rays, while Kenny and X-Ray became the main players at Starr's bar. The old adage "three's a crowd" certainly held true in this business arrangement. It didn't help that Sprackman had "inherited" his two partners when the Starr family recruited him.

For the first eleven years, from 1984 to 1995, X-Ray booked the bands while Sprackman focused on the other day-to-day operations that went into running a bar. In 1995, Yvonne Matsell, who had been booking shows for Kenny over at the Ultrasound, was brought over to the Horseshoe to help out X-Ray. There was some bitterness between the two, but X-Ray understood that his musical tastes were not keeping up with the times and what the audiences wanted.

In 1999, X-Ray decided to finally leave the business for good; he agreed to sell his Horseshoe shares to Jeff Cohen, the current majority owner whose story will be told in a later chapter.

But before we get to that, we should hear about the rise of the iconic Canadian roots rock band that helped establish a new Queen Street scene and a roots rock revival.

7

Rockabilly and a Roots Rock Revival

Here on the outskirts of life
Dreams seldom come true
Flippin' through photographs emotional holographs
Cutouts of all the figures you might've been
Reflections of a life which you once lived
— Blue Rodeo (Keelor/Cuddy), "Outskirts"

QUEEN STREET CIRCA 1984 was a hangout for musicians and art students. Think of it as the 1960s Yorkville coffee house scene for a new generation. Thanks largely to the cheap housing due to the recession, there was a rise in places for musicians to play and rehearse and artists to paint, perform, and just hang out along Queen West. Everyone knew each other, and there was a real DIY ethos and activist attitude among the resident artists and musicians. Some of the bands who emerged from this milieu included Martha and the Muffins, Cowboy Junkies, the Government, Rough Trade, and the Parachute Club. That spirit defined the passions and pursuits of Queen West's cultural life. "It was a very do-it-yourself [time]," explains Lorraine Segato, singer and guitarist for pop-dance band the Parachute Club, when asked to recall this moment in time in a recent interview. "That's an activist stance right there, like, 'I don't have funding or money but will do it anyway.' There was a lot of cross-pollination and fertilization of each other's projects just to get the work done, and that also fed into this idea of community. It made the community strong."

Besides the Horseshoe Tavern, this burgeoning musical community included the Rivoli (an ultra-hip music bar and comedy showcase where

The Kids in the Hall first performed); the BamBoo (a prime place for reggae and dub poetry); the Beverley Tavern (an art-punk haven, and the birthplace of the Elvis Monday Indie Music Showcase, which helped launch more than a few careers and later continued at the 'Shoe); the Rex (chic, hip, avant-garde jazz and blues bar); and the Cameron House (where cowpunk pioneer Handsome Ned lived and held court). All these venues were located in the short stretch of street from just west of Spadina to University Avenue.

All this added competition was good news for the 'Shoe. Many of the musicians, pub-crawlers, and outsiders were students from the Ontario College of Art (OCA), which changed its name to what most know it as today — OCAD — in 1996. At the same time, campus radio stations increased their wattage and started playing more local, indie rock, new wave, and punk bands. Also, after-hours clubs were really important due to the Prohibition-style provincial government at the time, which implemented new liquor bylaws where you couldn't drink past 9:00 p.m. unless you were eating food. The booze cans gave rise to a fresh and energetic street culture on Queen Street that previously had been dormant.

The Beverley Tavern, an "art-punk haven" and birthplace of the Elvis Monday Indie Music Showcase.

Mary Margaret O'Hara, an OCA art student at the time and a singer who has since recorded with the likes of Bruce Cockburn, Morrissey, and Neko Case, found homes at the Beverley and BamBoo during the early 1980s. Reminiscing about the spontaneity of this scene years later, she said, "It just seemed like at any time of day, you could just feel so excited, and things were happening, and you didn't care about making a cent."

Lorraine Segato recalls how the Parachute Club's original drummer, Billy Bryans, once rolled his drum kit up and down the street playing gigs from "the Rex to the Beverley to the Cameron to the BamBoo." He'd play in an art band here and a reggae band there, and then in the Parachute Club. "That was just a metaphor for the way everybody operated back then," Segato adds. Each club had a very different vibe, from punk to new wave to eclectic sounds that reflected Toronto's urban multiculturalism. Bryans's experience was a microcosm for what made Queen Street and its burgeoning arts scene so unique.

A sense of family was also fostered. "You used to be able to walk down Queen Street and you knew everybody, in every bookstore, every restaurant. I don't know how that works in this day and age. When you've got buildings that are moving upwards in the sky … it's hard to connect with people in a day-to-day way, one-on-one."

Blue Rodeo's Greg Keelor played the Horseshoe for the first time during the early 1980s in the band he and Jim Cuddy had at the time called the Hi-Fi's. The pair then decided to move to New York City in the fall of 1981 because, according to Keelor, the Toronto music scene had disappeared. Many of his musical heroes had moved to the States to "make it," so he figured, *Why not give it a shot, too?*

After three years in the megalopolis, he and Cuddy came home. Keelor recalls the seminal arts scene on Queen that greeted them when they returned in 1984:

> You felt like you were on the fringe of the juggernaut of Toronto. When we started playing down there, there was this little oasis that was Queen Street West where like-minded bohemians hung out. There was a lot of cross-fertilization. You had painters hanging out with writers, hanging out with musicians, hanging out with nihilists,

hanging out with punks … all these different people that usually wouldn't hang out together were hanging out at places like the Beverley, Peter Pan and the Parrot. It was a great scene. Scenes are always great when they start. There is something special when something like that happens, and then they just live out their timetable.

After Cuddy and Keelor returned from the Big Apple in the spring of 1984, it wasn't long before they assembled a new band and changed their name from Fly to France to Blue Rodeo. The new band's first gig back in their old hometown was not at the Horseshoe Tavern, but rather at the Rivoli on February 12, 1985. That gig was a sellout, according to Cuddy, which was a shock to him and the rest of the band, because they had just formed Blue Rodeo and nobody knew their sound yet. The reason for the full house was thanks largely to the aforementioned artistic oasis on Queen Street and a growing outlaw country fan base fuelled by Handsome Ned. It also helped that others in this underground scene, like Keith Demic (of the Demics), who Cuddy says was "the tastemaker on the street," and other former punk rockers from The Garys' days booking the 'Shoe endorsed the band. "That was the phenomena of that scene," he recalls. "The punks came back and came back in a different form. People came out of the woodwork, and the clubs were receptive to the music. It was the perfect storm and a very nurturing scene … it was the exact opposite of every other previous scene, since it was self-sustaining and not dictated by the agents or the managers."

Cuddy says Blue Rodeo's initial success was due to hard work and pounding the pavement without any help from the industry. The band played at all the bars along the Queen Street strip — from the Rivoli and the Beverley to the Horseshoe and the BamBoo. They saved fifty dollars from each gig (where they were making about four hundred dollars a night for the whole band) to print promotional posters that they handed out to the three daily newspapers — the *Toronto Star*, *Globe and Mail*, and *Toronto Sun* — and radio stations in the city. "We were all bonded in our love of what we were doing without any aspirations of it being anything else," Cuddy adds.

John Caton fell in love with Blue Rodeo after hearing the band play at the Horseshoe one night, and for a while there was not much else he could think about. He still remembers with fondness the first time he saw Cuddy,

Keelor, and the rest of the roots rock band play. Reflecting back, he says that time in the 1980s was an incredible period that he feels lucky to have been a part of. Today, Caton works in the tourism industry and lives in Campbell River, a city on British Columbia's coast; he hasn't been involved in the music industry for decades. But another lifetime ago, he was an artist manager and publisher. The day he heard Blue Rodeo for the first time was the day he was set to quit the music business for good — or, at least that's what he told his wife before heading down to that musical shrine at Queen and Spadina to hear what, for him, was still an unknown band, despite their having a growing following.

Caton had been working in the record business for Spontaneous Productions, managing the Arrows, a Canadian new wave band signed to A&M Records. The band's debut album *Stand Back* (1984) was a national success and included a top forty hit with "Meet Me in the Middle." The Arrows even toured that year as the opening act on the U.K. leg of Chris de Burgh's tour. The band, and Caton, worked out of a space in an old garment building that included office and rehearsal space. As many before him have learned, success in the music industry is fickle and fleeting. A business disagreement between Caton and his partner not long after that successful European tour for the Arrows meant that the young music manager found himself out of a job.

Around the same time, two of Caton's good friends, Richard Kruk and X-Ray MacRae, were involved in relaunching the Horseshoe Tavern. Seeing their buddy out of work, they offered him a job. "Those guys said, 'Come on over here,'" Caton recalls. "'Bring your desk and all your stuff, and we will set you up in an office in the basement of the Horseshoe. Come work with us and help us book acts.'"

Caton didn't need much convincing. He made himself at home in the 'Shoe's lower level, decking out his office with all his furniture: 1940s couches, Persian carpets, antique wooden gramophones. "It became a nice hangout for all of us," he says.

He admits those early days of trying to revive the Horseshoe were a struggle. Kruk and X-Ray were flying by the seats of their pants, not quite sure what the right formula was to turn the venue around. This was shortly before Starr brought Sprackman on board, and the bar still wasn't generating a lot of money. Caton admits they had to do some stuff under the table. "At times, we couldn't even afford to stock the bars with everything we needed," he reveals. "So every morning and every night, we would go over to Kruk's other bar [Crooks] and take some of the liquor, and bring it back to the Horseshoe and sell it there!"

With little money coming in, the Horseshoe was initially more of a sideline for Caton. He also had a real estate licence and had taken on a project out in Whitby, Ontario, selling homes for a new 1,800-lot subdivision. From noon until 8:00 p.m. every day, he would put on his sales hat, schmooze, and sell homes. This was right at a boom time for real estate, following the crash from 1983 to 1984. He estimates they were selling ten to fifteen homes a day and making really good money, so he could afford to come down to the 'Shoe at night and "dabble."

After many years in the music industry, Caton had his pulse on the scene: he knew all the new bands and acts that were coming up and playing other clubs north and south on Spadina, like the El Mocambo and Grossman's Tavern. The booking formula X-Ray used at the time was to bring in marquee bands on the weekend. The new managers were determined to have live music six nights a week, but it was a tough slog from the start. Mondays through Wednesdays were dead. The plan was to start bringing in some of the exciting stuff that was percolating on Queen Street. While the weekend saw more established artists, the early part of the week was offered to bands who played more or less for a case of beer. It gave them a chance to practise their stuff on a real stage.

Enter Blue Rodeo. One Monday, X-Ray told Caton that he had a new band with a varied background coming in to play. They'd recently dropped off their tape, and they sounded interesting. After a full day of selling homes up in Whitby, Caton sped down the highway to the Horseshoe, arriving right in the middle of the band's first set. He sat down at the bar next to X-Ray. Immediately, he was drawn to the band's psychedelic-tinged country-rock sound. "I was like, *Wow, these guys have got some incredible songs; the songwriting is phenomenal!*"

After their first set, the band came over to the bar to get their beer tickets, made some small talk, and then went back to the stage. Caton remained in a trance and listened to the rest of their set. "If the band wasn't exciting for me, I would usually get there at 10 p.m. and be gone halfway through their first set," he says. "That particular night, I stayed until they broke down their gear.... I wanted to talk to them."

Caton approached Cuddy and Keelor, Blue Rodeo's leaders, and over a couple of beers told them about his background in the music industry and about managing the Arrows. He wanted to know if they had a management or publishing deal. He saw the incredible potential in their songwriting. Initially, the guys were not that impressed with his spiel. You see, by this point, the pair had already become jaded with the so-called music industry and promises from agents, managers, and record companies. They had already fled the city for three years to live in New York and try their luck there after no one had given their music the time of day in their hometown. Caton still recalls their reaction to his initial proposal:

> They were like, "Don't even come to us with that shit. We've been around the block; we've been flown to France, the works. We're just back from New York City where we tried to get deals. By now, we've listened to every huckster that calls themselves a manager. We've resigned ourselves to the fact that we are just going to play music for fun. Music as a career? Fuck it. It's never going to happen, so we are not even interested. We all have day jobs and plan to just play on the weekends from now on."

As he drove up the Don Valley Parkway and then east along Highway 401 home to Whitby that night, all Caton could think about were those songs. The beautiful melodies, wistful words, and heartfelt harmonies between Cuddy and Keelor replayed over and over again in his mind. Bazil Donovan, the band's bassist, says you've got to hear Caton's wife retell this story: "She says he came in the door and then she asked, 'How did it go tonight, did you clean out your office?' And he said, 'I saw this band tonight.' [She] looked in his eyes and could tell he hadn't quit the business … hadn't given up yet."

Wives tend to have the best instincts in reading their husbands, and she definitely was right on this occasion. Caton wasn't finished yet trying to woo Blue Rodeo. They were too good a band to let go, and they became his pet project. He just had a feeling. First, a plan was needed, along with a more convincing proposal. He knew he would have to take it slow. A few days later, he got hold of Cuddy and Keelor. His pitch: *Don't think about this proposal as packing the band and all your gear in a van and going on the road.*

"Think first about your songs," Caton told them, using his most persuasive real estate agent voice that had worked so well in his other life. "They are great, and I really believe there is money for you guys to make in publishing." The answer was still no. As Cuddy explains: "We never ever wanted a publishing deal. When we were in New York, songwriter Garland Jeffreys told us, 'whatever you do, keep your publishing.'"*

Flash ahead another couple of weeks: The Horseshoe had booked the band back for another night. Behind the scenes, X-Ray and Caton started to hatch a plan to show Blue Rodeo that they meant business. The idea was to get hold of all the music business contacts they collectively knew and fill the place with a bunch of record industry heavy hitters. And that's exactly what the pair did. They worked the phones and called all the industry insiders they knew. That fateful Monday night arrived. The 'Shoe was jammed with about 250 people. Blue Rodeo was dumbstruck with the makeup of the audience that night. After the show Cuddy and Keelor went over to Caton, and bluntly Keelor said, "What the fuck? Where did all these industry people come from?"

Caton's plan had obviously succeeded. The boys in the band were ready to listen to his proposals. The following day, after another stint selling houses, he met them at the Montreal Bistro, a popular jazz venue on Sherbourne Street that eventually closed in 2006 after twenty-five years of operation. Over the course of dinner and drinks, a meeting of the minds came together among the trio; Blue Rodeo signed a management deal with Caton, but as mentioned, they wisely kept their publishing. With a passionate manager behind them, they were now thinking that taking one more shot at making a demo wasn't such a bad idea. Caton arranged for his good friend producer Terry Brown (who was known for his work with Rush, but he had also worked with the likes of The Who when he lived in England) to come out to the Horseshoe the next time the band played and capture their sound to tape, live off the floor. A mobile recording truck was brought into the 'Shoe during the day, and a ten-song demo was recorded and then later mixed at Sounds Interchange. Once mastered, the demo was shopped around to various record companies.

Nobody was interested.

---

* To this day, Blue Rodeo owns the publishing rights to all of their songs.

*   *   *

Neither Caton and his partners nor the band were ready to call it quits and give up on their dream of landing a record deal just yet: "We came back, and I said to the others, 'We need to make a better recording and do it ourselves … we might as well form a production company with the band.'"

Risque Disque was born. First, Caton, Brown, and MacRae formed a management consulting company for their production work; then, Caton, Brown, and Blue Rodeo formed Risque Disque. "The whole name came out of the risk of doing something independent," Caton says. "In those days, being independent was a hard scenario."

Caton had so much faith in Blue Rodeo's music that he felt the inherent risk of this new business venture was worth it. After cutting a more sophisticated demo, they made the rounds to three of the major record companies of the day again: A&M, CBS, and WEA (Warner Bros.). All three were interested, but Dave Tollington, vice-president of WEA, and Bob Roper, artists and repertoire manager at WEA Canada, won.

Ironically, it had been Roper who had passed on a previous demo Cuddy and Keelor, then known as Fly to France, had recorded with a New Zealand band called the Drongos. The tape had contained four songs: "Try," "Floating," "Outskirts," and "Rose-Coloured Glasses." In the book *Have Not Been the Same: The CanRock Renaissance 1985–1995*, Cuddy recalls Roper's earlier rejection. The note from the A&R man said, "I felt that the songs were well crafted and presented in a pop vein that was too soft for our current direction. At the time, I am only developing much harder-edged rock artists who are currently touring live on a national base." Just one more sign of how quickly tastes can change in the music industry.

Risque Disque sat down with Warner and signed a worldwide production deal. That's how it all started for the band — and it all started at the Horseshoe Tavern. Remembering those 'Shoe days, Cuddy says, "It had the right stage and the right scene. X-Ray and Kenny were the right guys running it. We were so shocked that we had an audience from the beginning. The Horseshoe became our de facto home. It was fun to have a bar where you had automatic entrance. It was crowded, we could walk by the line, and they would say, 'come on in. go down to the basement and see the guys: X-Ray, Kenny, and John.' It was all enjoyable stuff."

Risque Disque went on to sign other bands like Crash Vegas, Basic English, and Scott Dibble; the business was all based around the 'Shoe. Caton and crew continued to operate out of the dingy office in the basement of the bar. "Our business model was based on the fact that we had a venue and we had these acts that we could develop, nurture, and grow."

In the weeks and months before the band landed the international record deal with Warner, Caton says they had to "prove and sell to the industry that this cowpunk, left-of-field, Everly-Brothers-meets-The-Clash type of stuff they were doing was the real deal." At the time, the only Canadian bands that record companies were signing were post–new wave craze hair bands like Platinum Blonde. As much as the demo tape convinced the music industry executives, they also couldn't ignore a band that had such an incredible following at the city's most iconic music venue. As Caton tells it:

> Blue Rodeo performed first on Monday nights. As they brought in more people, they started playing on Wednesdays, then Thursdays, until they were regularly filling the place.… At that point, we started booking them for three straight nights: Thursday through Saturday. The place would be full, and there would be lineups one hundred people deep, waiting on the sidewalk, all the way down to the Black Bull, all desperately wanting to get in. We started with a five-dollar cover charge and gradually increased it to twenty. The demand for the band in Toronto was huge. This was just before we had the record deal.

Risque Disque took this same development and booking model across the country. Since Blue Rodeo's original drummer, Cleave Anderson, worked as a mail carrier for Canada Post, he couldn't travel until after all his deliveries were complete. Cleave would be finished work by 1:00 p.m. on a Friday, and the band would be on a plane to Vancouver that afternoon, where they would play a pair of gigs on the weekend at the Railway Club. Slowly, the band built up the same buzz there as they had back in T.O. Once they had an audience of faithful fans in Vancouver, they moved on to Canada's other major music centres: Edmonton, Calgary, and Halifax. "Every time we went back to the Horseshoe, there were huge lines and the cover charge kept going higher and higher and higher as the demand grew," Caton says.

Jim Cuddy (*left*) and Greg Keelor play the Horseshoe with Blue Rodeo in 1986.

Not long after Blue Rodeo and Risque Disque signed with Warner Bros. Records, the demand for the management team grew. Caton and his colleagues had to hire more staff to run the office, so the cramped quarters in the Horseshoe's basement were no longer big enough. Risque Disque moved over to Draper Street — a one-way street between Front and Wellington — into a historic brownstone row house that was once the officer quarters for soldiers stationed at Fort York. While the label eventually folded with Caton exiting the music business, in 2016, Risque Disque Records, now based in Nanaimo on Vancouver Island, relaunched and rebranded with a set of new releases.

* * *

If there were a king of that seminal Queen Street scene — a ringleader of the artistic circus on the outskirts — it was Handsome Ned. Upon returning to Toronto from New York City, Blue Rodeo gravitated to the Queen Street scene led by, and centred on, Ned (née Robin Masyk). After a stint of his

Cowpunk pioneer Handsome Ned was the leader of the roots rock scene on Queen Street West in the early 1980s; he lived and held court at the Cameron House down the street, but he also played the Horseshoe. Here he is at the 'Shoe with his first band, the Velours, in 1981.

own south of the border with his brother, in Austin, Texas, the ex–punk rocker had also returned to Toronto, bringing with him the outlaw country music and rockabilly tradition he had been turned on to in the Lone Star State. While in Texas, one of his claims to fame was playing at the Broken Spoke, the legendary honky-tonk where Hank Williams, Ernest Tubb, and Bob Wills used to play. Back in Toronto, Ned, always wearing his trademark ten-gallon hat and a sheepish grin, found a home at the Cameron House, one block west of Spadina. He played this new brand of cowpunk for anyone who would listen. He once had a rule that he wouldn't perform until there were more than ten people in the audience. Come they did to listen to Ned's musical sermons — even though country music was far from popular at the time. "Ned was the king," Keelor told the authors of *Have Not Been the Same.* "He was a scenester."

Every Saturday for five years, starting on January 9, 1982, Ned did a matinee in the Cameron's backroom. By 1984, when Keelor returned to Hogtown, Ned's Saturday matinee was the meeting point, social hub, and watering hole for many in that influential Queen Street Scene —poets, artists, musicians, aspiring actors.

Keelor describes these weekly shows, when the place was packed to the rafters:

> It was a drunkard's dream, a great collection of artists, musicians, drug addicts, and writers. He would start around 4:00 p.m. and leave only when the nighttime band kicked him off the stage. We all knew these were "good times" — a strange sense of community and creativity. Half in the bag, you would look high on the wall of the front bar to the inscription that read "This is Paradise," and you would smile.

Blue Rodeo met their first drummer, Cleave Anderson, to discuss joining their new band at the Metropolitan Restaurant on Yonge Street as he celebrated the birth of his first child, Tristan. Rounding out their outfit was bassist Bazil "Baz" Donovan, who had been playing in a variety of bands in the country bars farther west on Queen Street — places like the Parkdale Tavern, the Drake Hotel, the Gladstone, and the Claremont — for nearly a decade. He'd also spent a lot of time in his twenties playing the famed after-hours club the Matador. More recently, he had played in the Sharks with Anderson and Sherry Kean.

Donovan has a long history with the Horseshoe. His parents saw many of the Grand Ole Opry stars there in the 1960s. In 1973, Bazil played there for the first time; he was only eighteen when he joined a country gospel band called Cliff Carroll and the Hitchhikers. At the time, Baz was into country music, but he didn't love it. Rock was his passion. Words of advice from one of Donovan's uncles, who was a gigging guitarist, served the bassist well and also maybe played a role in him answering the infamous ad Cuddy and Keelor placed in *NOW Magazine* looking for a bassist for Blue Rodeo:[*]

> I was into country music, but didn't love it. I loved rock. I played it because I was able to play it and it was a better

---

[*] The story of how Blue Rodeo's co-founders Cuddy and Keelor recruited a bassist for their new band is now part of the fabric of Canadian music history lore. Upon returning to Toronto in the spring of 1984, the pair placed an ad in the Toronto alternative weekly *NOW Magazine*. It read: "If you've dropped acid at least 20 times, lost three or four years to booze and looking good, and can still manage to keep time, call Jim or Greg."

way of earning a living than working in a factory, which I did for a while and that was horrible. My uncle once told me, "You are going to have to wear many hats in this business." He was realistic: "It doesn't matter what haircut you have to wear as long as you are playing. Just get out there and do it. Play with a wig or stupid suit. Just do it." Those words always rang in my head.

Later, the flashy, eccentric keyboardist Bobby Wiseman rounded out the band's original lineup.

Cuddy and Keelor's second-ever gig back in town ended up being an opening slot for Handsome Ned at the Horseshoe on Valentine's Day, 1985. A twenty-four-track mobile recording truck was set up, and veteran producer Terry Brown was hired to capture the show. The magic of that Handsome Ned set was never heard until more than three decades later because the recording costs were never paid. Former Horseshoe Tavern part owner and booker X-Ray MacRae kept the tapes and stored them at his farmhouse in Napanee. Thanks to an encounter years later with Ned's brother Jim Masyk, this six-song EP of lost live recordings, which includes the previously unissued original "Little Miss Lonely Heart," was remixed, remastered, and released in January 2017 by Cameron House Records as *The Handsome Neds: Live at the Horseshoe*. Ned and many of his followers found paradise at the Cameron and the other bars along the Queen Street strip during those few years. Unfortunately, this paradise was soon lost — for some.

Flash forward two years: In 1987 Blue Rodeo, inspired by Ned's spirit, hit the studio and cut their first record for Warner Canada — the appropriately titled *Outskirts*, since that's whence musical outlaws always take their muses; it's also where their followers and fans live. Within a year, this major-label debut had sold more than one hundred and fifty thousand copies in Canada and garnered the band a ton of hardware, including Song of the Year from the Canadian Music Publishers Association for the ballad "Try" and five *RPM* Big Country Awards, to name just two honours. At the 1989 Junos, the band cleaned up: winning three of the five categories in which they were nominated.

Unfortunately, Ned was not around to witness his friends' success. As with many musicians before and after him, a heroin addiction took its toll, and the drugs won the battle. He passed away on January 10, 1987, of a suspected drug overdose, on the eve of what would have been his five-year anniversary playing the matinee at the Cameron House and six months shy of his thirtieth birthday. His death, to a degree, marked the end of that seminal Queen Street Scene. As Jim Cuddy recalls, "We started making *Outskirts* on January 8, the day my son was born; Ned died our second day in the studio on January 10." In *Have Not Been the Same*, Cuddy sums up the significance of what Ned's death meant: "It was definitely an end to the scene as we had known it. It certainly wasn't innocent anymore, and the stakes were higher because some people got a contract and others broke up — but certain things had been determined that for the longest time had been so gloriously undetermined."

8

The Early Nineties

Crazy days are crazy days indeed
I'm wondering when I'll come down from this peak
— The Watchmen, "Crazy Days," from *McLaren Furnace Room* (1992)

AS THE 1980S MADE WAY for the 1990s, Blue Rodeo had grown too big for the Horseshoe Tavern. They moved on to the Diamond Club and bigger and bigger concert halls until they were selling out Massey Hall. All these years later, they still hold a piece of the 'Shoe in their hearts and are grateful to the owners — and to the fans — who believed in them and supported them from the beginning.

Blue Rodeo's success sparked a new explosion of indie bands — from both Toronto and other parts of Canada — who saw that with hard work, dedication, and, of course, a little luck of the ol' Horseshoe, they, too, might strike it big. If there is any one person who can lay claim to helping many of the next generation of rock bands climb the ladder of success, it's Ralph James. The music man once played bass in the late-seventies rock band Harlequin, but in the early 1990s he was working for the Agency, assigned to the Horseshoe Tavern — a venue, he says, no agent wanted to touch because of the owners' reputation for disliking people in his profession. Brimming with an unrivalled passion for the music industry, James was undaunted; he used the venue to launch many bands and give them their shot at stardom. Names like the Watchmen, Nickelback, Billy Talent, and the Trews are just a few of the bands James helped, thanks to a relationship he built with the owners of the Horseshoe Tavern that continues to this day.

Jack Starr, the man who started it all back in 1947, enjoying retirement — spending time with his grandchildren.

He is currently an agent and chief executive officer in the Toronto office of United Talent Agency, which bought out the Agency Group Canada in 2015.

"People who come to the 'Shoe for the first time say it's a dive," James says. "But it's a great dive. One of the great things about the Horseshoe is that they've always understood the industry part of their persona ... they know who all the key people are at the record labels, the agents, and the agencies, and they are always accommodating."

When James was first assigned to book bands from the Agency into the legendary tavern, the reputation of X-Ray and Sprackman and their dislike of agents had already made its way to him. "I was given the thankless task of dealing with X-Ray," James says. "I came down [there] every night for three or four nights in a row, and he wouldn't see me."

How did James eventually win over the talent buyer? X-Ray invited him to his office in the dungeon, a.k.a. the 'Shoe's basement, to give him the ground rules: "I walked into his office, and on his desk he had this stack of unsigned contracts. He said to me, 'I don't sign contracts. It's just my word. You take the door, and we take the bar.'"

Former part owner X-Ray MacRae (*left*) with legendary rock guitarist Link Wray — the inventor of the power chord, circa 1998.

That formula worked for James. He was sure his bands could fill the bar. And his artists did, every weekend, starting with acts like Paul James, the Razorbacks, and the Downchild Blues Band. "I signed all those bands," he says, proudly. "In our old booking system, do you know how many pages the 'Shoe fills? Hundreds."

Today, he's got nothing but accolades for X-Ray and Sprackman, and their successors Jeff Cohen and Craig Laskey. "They are all awesome," James comments. "They've given so many bands their chance. If you haven't played there, you've probably missed a step in your career. They've always kept developing talent and believing there was a reason to develop talent, most of it Canadian. There are some people I work with who call me a shareholder here, which I am not, but I feel like I am, because I feel like they are shareholders in my emerging establishment."

*   *   *

Another band that owes a debt of gratitude for their music career to both James and the Horseshoe is the Watchmen. The Winnipeg band was one of the first groups Ralph James signed when he became an agent. He was their biggest ally then, and still is today. When the Watchmen first came to Toronto, they played bars like Cadillac Jacks' over on Adelaide but nobody showed up. X-Ray finally gave the band a chance, based on James's glowing words. It was on a Tuesday night, and there were maybe half a dozen people there, but all of a sudden the buzz went around town and the crowd multiplied. X-Ray then booked them at the Horseshoe for a month-long residency. Before long, the band was selling the place out and there were lineups to get in to their shows every weekend.

Joey Serlin, the band's guitarist, says that for someone who grew up in Winnipeg, playing the 'Shoe was a definite sign they had arrived. "Just playing that room was something to be proud about and tell all your friends back home," Serlin says. "We had some really special shows there. Kenny and X-Ray were really nice to us. They gave us a residency."

Serlin recalls staying in a "horrible hotel" in Chinatown called The Grange for a month while gigging at the 'Shoe and a few other bars around town. Eventually, after they had honed their sound and built up their fan base, James arranged for Jake Gold and Allan Gregg, partners in the Management Trust (who signed the Tragically Hip to their first management deal) to see the Watchmen play at the Horseshoe. The band drove up to Toronto from Winnipeg specifically for the occasion.

When asked about this particular show twenty-five years later, Serlin remembers it as if it were yesterday: "After the show, we were hanging out backstage and Jake and Allan come up to us and say, 'We are going to sign you guys; we want to represent you.' Well, we got back in our van and we were on a high and up the entire drive back to Winnipeg. That was the beginning of our career." Adds lead singer Danny Greaves, "That drive was pretty memorable. We had made it to the next level. That night was the beginning of it."

That Horseshoe gig set the stage for the Watchmen's inspiring indie debut *McLaren Furnace Room* (1992), named in honour of their rehearsal space in the basement of Winnipeg's McLaren Hotel. A year later, the album was picked up by MCA, who rereleased it, giving it wider distribution and acclaim. This eventually led to the record being certified gold in Canada by

The Watchmen.

the Canadian Recording Industry Association on March 6, 1996, for selling more than fifty thousand copies. "That set the table for our career that followed," says Serlin. "All that stuff happened at the 'Shoe."

Later, when the band reunited in 2010, the Horseshoe was a natural fit and one of the first venues they played. What is it about the 'Shoe for Serlin that makes it such a magical place? "It's the ghosts of the people who have played there before you," he says. "There is definitely a weight. It's like if you play the Grand Ole Opry. There's the weight and the history that is always there. With that comes a responsibility to deliver, which we've wanted to do every time we've played [there]."

*   *   *

Steve Stanley, ex-guitarist and original member of the Lowest of the Low, doesn't recall the first time he played the Horseshoe Tavern, but he does remember going to places like the Turning Point, Larry's Hideaway, and the Cabana Room to see bands when he was underage. When the Lowest of the

Low first started playing shows around Toronto in 1990, they signed on to play a three-night stint once a month for a year at a small bar called the Blue Moon.

"That was when we really started to do our DIY thing and build our audience," Stanley recalls. "We took the indie route when no one else was doing it that way. It just happened at a time when we didn't expect it and nobody expected it. We did it for nine months. Then we started to play the Ultrasound — where Kenny and X-Ray were involved. At that point, we considered the Horseshoe the holy grail."

Stanley says that he stalked X-Ray in those days:

> I would go down there in the day over and over again. The first time we met downstairs in his office, he listened and didn't really say much. The second time he agreed to meet, I had probably been there four or five times by then with my spiel: "I don't know if you've heard of our band, we've done this, this and this, and we'd like to play here." I remember catching him downstairs by the washrooms and it was obvious he was perturbed that I kept bugging him. I'll never forget this line for my whole life. He turns to me and says, "Yeah, yeah, you'll get your chance, but here's something you've got to understand: every dog gets their day." He was basically saying, *You guys are not playing here.*

Persistence eventually paid off, though; it wasn't long after X-Ray delivered that epigram to Stanley that the Lowest of the Low found the holy grail and were booked into the Horseshoe. It helped that Yvonne Matsell, who had already brought the band into the Ultrasound, put in a good word to Kenny and X-Ray. Quickly, they graduated from playing early in the week to playing full weekends at the Horseshoe circa 1992. Ron Hawkins, Stanley's bandmate in Lowest of the Low, who still leads the group today, recalls that some of the band's earliest gigs at the 'Shoe coincided with the Toronto Blue Jays appearing in the World Series. "We were set to go onstage at 10:30 p.m. and the ballgame was still on," Hawkins recalls. "I remember I told X-Ray, 'If you put us on now, people are going to kill us or throw bottles at us!' We survived that night by waiting it out."

By 1992, the Lowest of the Low's persistence paid off and the band was gigging regularly at the Horseshoe. Pictured here is Ron Hawkins in one of the band's shows in more recent years.

Stanley recalls the band at that time was also conscious to a fault of not overstepping its size, turning down gigs that were on a bigger scale because they wanted to follow the same model of heroes of theirs like Billy Bragg. "The biggest he got was playing to venues of one thousand seats," says Stanley. "None of us loved the idea of playing concerts in arenas. I remember we turned down a five-night stand playing the PNE in Vancouver opening for Bryan Adams because none of us liked him. In hindsight, it probably didn't make sense, but we were always aware of wanting to play places where we could still connect with the audience."

And connect with an audience is exactly what The Low did at the Horseshoe. In the years since, the band has split and reunited time and again, and they've always come back to play the Horseshoe Tavern, especially to help the venue and its faithful patrons celebrate some of its major anniversaries. When the Lowest of the Low broke up for the first time in 1995, Stanley did his first solo show there at Dave Bookman's Nu Music Night.

Beyond The Low and his solo gigs, one of his most unforgettable nights at the Horseshoe happened on a Sunday around 2009. Stanley had been sitting at home when the phone rang. It was the Horseshoe's booking agent, Craig Laskey. He said, "Steve, what are you doing? Do you want to see a show tonight? Here's the thing: Peter Buck [of R.E.M.] is in town with the Baseball Project, and their gear got held up at the border. Can we borrow your guitars?" Stanley gave the band his Les Paul, his Gretsch, and his Telecaster. "That was so cool," he remembers. "They all used my guitars that night. That is a weird thing when I think about that. Your guitars are very personal, but I gave them to them without a second thought."

*   *   *

In 2010, about six months after Pat Burns, Toronto Maple Leafs coach from 1992 to 1995, died, Mike Keenan, who was a great friend of Pat's, wanted to do a tribute to him at the Horseshoe Tavern. He contacted Dave Bidini, and Dave put together a band. The tribute night in honour of Burns's memory featured covers of Neil Young and Gordon Lightfoot songs. Stanley reminisces about this evening: "We did our twelve songs, then one by one these guys came up to join us. Pat Burns's best friend did a song that went on for like twenty minutes. It was a magical night. The Burns family was all there, and there were all these hockey guys. Glenn Healy, with an entire pipe band of twenty-two guys, piped everyone in to start off the show. Tie Domi was there, too, and gave a speech."

*   *   *

Tuesdays at the Horseshoe were always a tough sell. First, it was the night when many people went out for cheap movies. Second, it wasn't quite mid-week yet, so if there was one night concertgoers decided to stay in, Tuesday was usually the one they picked.

Dave "Bookie" Bookman, a musician who played in a variety of bands in the 1980s, was also a radio personality at the indie rock station CFNY. As a musician, he recalls always feeling the Horseshoe had a real reverence to it. "While there were other clubs you would play, when you went to the Horseshoe, you knew you were somewhere special, and it was different." On Kenny and X-Ray, he says, "They were a little intimidating."

In 1993, Yvonne Matsell was booking bands at Ultrasound, the music bar upstairs at X-Ray's restaurant at Duncan and Queen. She was also helping to book bands at the Horseshoe. The pressure to fill nights was getting to her. One day, she asked Bookman if he knew of any bands that she could hire. She was going to see bands all the time, but she was getting worn out. She told him, "If I could stay home and a band could play my living room, I would be happy." Bookie listened to Matsell's predicament and figured he could help: "Instead of you chasing bands, why not give me one night a week and I'll book the bands for you that I want to see?" Nu Music Night was born. The concept: Give local, unknown bands an opportunity to play for free, on a slow night at the bar. This would give them some exposure and experience, and it would help the bar fill a slot on an otherwise slow night. The concept was similar to the popular Elvis Mondays started by William New of Groovy Religion in 1983 at the Beverley Tavern as a way to showcase indie bands. It later continued for many years at the newly renovated Drake Hotel.

"That was the template I used," says Bookman, "but I knew I had to put my own twist on it. First, I needed to come up with the right night. Monday was no good because of Monday Night Football. How about Tuesday?"

Matsell was sold. "Initially, I asked my friends for suggestions and booked bands I wanted to see, tying these Tuesday nights into a show I was doing at the time on The Edge called *The Indie Hour*," Bookman explains. "At first it was hard because I didn't know what I was doing … I was just figuring it out on the fly."

The first Nu Music Night was in November 1993. Once Matsell moved over to the Horseshoe Tavern full-time in 1995, she suggested Bookman bring the concept there. It was an easy sell to X-Ray and Kenny. From then on, Tuesday at the 'Shoe became known as Nu Music Night. Over the years, there have been so many memorable shows that have happened inside those sweaty walls early in the week — from Foo Fighters to Thom Yorke of Radiohead doing a solo set, from the Strokes to Linkin Park.

Even everyone's favourite Canadian hard rock band to ridicule — Alberta's Nickelback — who've gone on to become one of the country's most commercially successful bands, selling more than fifty million records worldwide, got their start at Bookie's Tuesday showcase. The band's agent, Ralph James, had the people fly in from Roadrunner Records to see them specifically, and after their Tuesday night set at the 'Shoe they got signed. Later, when they exploded, they returned and did a Tuesday for Bookie out of respect. "That's part of the magic of the 'Shoe," James says.

Over the years, Canadian bands wanting to hold a record release party or a warm-up gig before going on tour would call up Bookie and get him to pencil in a Tuesday Nu Music Night slot for them. Besides the music, the night is about community. "When we started it, this was an important event to get people back to the Horseshoe and see live music again," Bookman explains. "If you live in town, how do you get into the scene? You come down to the 'Shoe on Tuesday nights. The spirit is such that you are always going to meet people; it will be a friendly, open environment. It wasn't about selling new music, it was about selling a new attitude.

"Later, Elliott Lefko from MCA Concerts started throwing stuff our way on Tuesday nights. We really benefited from that relationship. That was the start of having all those alt-country bands like Wilco and Son Volt. We even got the first show Linkin Park ever played in Toronto as well as the first Strokes show in town."

As the aforementioned concerts illustrate, Bookie eventually evolved the Nu Music Nights beyond just bringing in local unknown acts on Tuesdays. The club started showcasing bands from out of town, too. Via word of mouth and friendships, they've kept the Nu Music Night going and growing. During the first year, Bookie says it was just him trying to come up with the lineups off the top of his head; they weren't tied in to what Cohen and Laskey were doing as part of their booking policies. But when they decided to make those Tuesdays and the philosophy behind them a central part of their vision, they launched a new generation at the Horseshoe and put their stamp on the venue. "That took a lot of pressure off of me," says Bookman. "It was now part of a whole thing. That was a great relief. If that hadn't happened, I doubt I could have made it grow."

And grow it certainly did — from unknown indie bands playing for free to some of the hippest alternative rock bands on the radio waves. "The day Radiohead's *The Bends* came out, lead singer Thom Yorke was in town," recalls Bookman. "It was 6:30 p.m. and I was interviewing him on the radio at CFNY. I asked him what he was doing that night and whether he wanted to come down to the Horseshoe and play some songs. He said yes! That was another night that was really incredible. Thom came down and played like five songs off *The Bends*, including 'High and Dry,' for like two hundred people at the Horseshoe."

Of all the Tuesday night shows, Bookman says Foo Fighters for him was the *pièce de résistance*.

The band [was] in town doing press for their third record and I figured there was nothing to lose. I had another band playing that night who were managed by the same label. When I met them at the radio station that morning, before I could say anything, they asked me, 'What about this Tuesday night thing you guys do? Why don't we come and play? I was like, *What!* The next thing you know, the Foo Fighters announce they were going to play Nu Music Night. It was all arranged behind my back; it freaked the whole city out, but it was amazing.

Did Bookman ever imagine that twenty-two years later, he would still be hosting Nu Music Nights at the Horseshoe? "Yes," he says, "because as long as we are all in this together, it will never stop. It will only stop when we all stop. This is what we do; this is our life. My job is fun, and I get to do it with my friends. This thing will be going on as long as we have it going. Hopefully we live forever. That's the spirit of it.

"It isn't about the money," Bookman adds. "It isn't about stardom; it's about sharing a stage together. If you didn't like the band that was on, there was another one up in half an hour."

* * *

Dave Bidini played the Horseshoe for the first time in 1983, opening for the Government on New Year's Eve. "That was pretty cool because back then the 'Shoe was still known as the freaky place, where freaky people went to do freaky things," says Bidini, guitarist for Rheostatics. "It certainly didn't have a populist reputation the way it does now. It was by no means the cool place to go. At that time it was the closest it got to being a dive bar: cheap bar and a small cover … it was a place where artists and weirdos could go and it still had the remnants of the punk days. It was thrilling for us to play there. I was crazy and partly terrified."

From the mid-1990s into the 2000s, Rheostatics, like so many bands before them, found a home at the Horseshoe. One of the more memorable moments was a Tuesday night in 1995. It was the first show Don Kerr played on drums after original member Dave Clark had left. Bidini recalls, "It was a big night for us because Dave had been a key member of the band and people were wondering what we were going to do next musically. We were all so fraught with nerves and anxiety.

"Around that time, we also started doing our residencies. We did some residencies at the old Ultrasound on Queen and Ted's Wrecking Yard, then we moved them permanently to the Horseshoe. We went ten in a row, eleven in a row, twelve in a row, thirteen in a row, fourteen in a row, and then back to thirteen the last time we did it. Every fall, we lived at that club for two weeks a year. People would come from everywhere in the world to see those shows. They would design their years around coming to the Horseshoe to see us play. That's pretty amazing."

How did this stretch of shows known as the "Fall Nationals" come to the 'Shoe? Ever since the Rheos had played the Underground in Ottawa in the mid-1980s at a show Jeff Cohen was promoting for the radio station, Bidini had kept in touch with him. When his old friend took over booking at the Horseshoe, it came at a time when Rheostatics were a bit burned out from the road and constantly touring. "We always went on tour and did two weeks here, two weeks there, so Jeff said why don't we do two weeks in the same place," Bidini recalls. "Jeff still asks about the Fall Nationals today. He is the one who named it. It never would have been too crazy an idea, but it was like, let's try it."

Unlike the sixties and seventies when the Nashville stars came to town and week-long residencies were the norm, that wasn't happening in the late eighties and into the nineties. Bidini recalls:

> We did the Fall Nationals too mainly because of Stompin' Tom Connors, who had played there ... it was a bit of a tip of the hat to him. We knew there was no way we could approach his record of twenty-five straight shows, but we wanted to give it a shot. It was a challenge for us to keep each show interesting; instead of going out and playing the same set, we would do different things — or try to — every night. We would also have different people play with us. One night would be a guest vocalist night where we would have twenty-four singers come up and sing twenty-four Rheostatics songs with us. It became the kind of thing where people would just show up unannounced with their instruments and play.

One of the great sequences of my life, around 2001, we did twelve nights in a row and two shows on the Sunday for a total of thirteen shows in twelve nights at the Horseshoe. I remember I got strep throat in the middle of that run, but I only missed one show. It was the last night and we played until 3:00 a.m. I had to get up at 7:00 a.m. to catch a flight to Mongolia of all places for this hockey movie that I was making. I remember going to the airport without any sleep feeling how lucky I was to be able to play in this great place, have these great shows with a great band, in front of great fans and great people and then have a kind of life that I was able to go and do these incredible exotic things while doing interesting things in music. I'm very fond of that night leaving the Horseshoe. I remember thinking the Horseshoe was a great place to go to, but it was also always a great place to leave because it sent you off … gave you a proper send-off in a lot of ways.

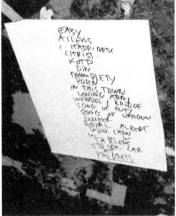

Next to Stompin' Tom Connors, beginning in the mid-1990s and into the 2000s nobody played the Horseshoe Tavern more than Rheostatics. Here they are on that storied stage on March 29, 2007.

One other story Bidini shares is about the night he was asked to open up for the Midi-Ogres, Dave Bookman's old band, who were opening up for Townes Van Zandt, of all people. He recalls this meeting with the legendary Texas singer-songwriter:

> I played, did sound check, then went downstairs to the dressing room and found myself there with Townes and Butch Hancock, who was playing drums in his band. Butchie started to play a song, Townes joined in, and the two of them were suddenly both playing their acoustic guitars. I was there with my drumsticks, so I started to play on a ceiling pipe, keeping time. People one by one started walking in to this jam session. Me, Townes, and Butch played for about half an hour together. It only hit me later ... what had happened that I had the chance to play with these two legends — particularly Townes — he later came up on stage to do his set and left after five songs to go back in the dressing room to find bits of alcohol that were left over in half-drunk beer bottles. He was in really rough shape at this point. My friend Gord Cumming and I went down to try to talk him into coming back on stage, which we did, but he came back and played just three songs. Being in such close proximity to such a great man, and being able to cross paths with him was an incredible thing. It's a place where you can find legends.

9

Secret Shows

Plus ça change, plus c'est la même chose.
— French critic Jean-Baptiste Alphonse Karr

THE FRENCH EPIGRAM CITED above is usually translated as "The more things change, the more they stay the same." The phrase suits the Horseshoe Tavern well. For while there have been numerous changes since Starr opened the tavern in 1947 — changes to the structure and the size of its footprint, changes in ownership, and changes in booking policies — the core values and spirit of what has made it legendary and a Canadian institution have remained the same for seventy years.

Another thing that has remained the same, and has come to be expected, is the unexpected. Walk through the doors at 370 Queen Street West on any given night, and you don't know what might happen by closing time.

The night The Band reunited on the stage at the Horseshoe certainly qualifies as one of those surprises. March 13, 1989, is a date that is forever etched in Kenny Sprackman's mind. Three of the four surviving original members of The Band — Rick Danko, Garth Hudson, and Robbie Robertson — were in Toronto for the Juno Awards. The Band was also being inducted into the Canadian Music Hall of Fame that year. Drummer Levon Helm was absent for the celebration, citing long-standing differences with Robertson as his reason not to take part in The Band's induction ceremony. The seminal band had formed in 1960 and first came to fame in Hogtown over on Yonge Street as part of Ronnie Hawkins's backing band at the famed Le Coq d'Or. They were the first North American band to appear on the cover of *Time* magazine, and in 2004 *Rolling Stone* named them one of the one hundred greatest artists of all time.

It was only natural that while they were in town they would play the Horseshoe. Sprackman says he used to book the reunited Band without Robbie Robertson. "They would play at the 'Shoe from time to time, but they hadn't played with Robbie for years," he recalls. In fact, Danko and Hudson had played with Robertson only once since the 1976 filming of their swan song *The Last Waltz*. That had been a New York City memorial gig for former bandmate Richard Manuel, who had passed away in 1986.

On that March night in Toronto, 250 lucky patrons packed the venue. Everybody but Robertson was up on the Horseshoe stage. Mid-set, Sprackman received a phone call from Reggie, the bar's well-known bouncer, telling him to meet him out back: "I go to the back door, and there's Reggie with Robbie [Robertson]. Robbie had his guitar in one hand and his amp in the other. He came through the door and walked up side stage."

Minutes before the 1:00 a.m. last call, Robertson quietly stepped onto the stage and to the microphone and joined his bandmates. The Horseshoe Tavern exploded. He struck the opening chords of "Life Is a Carnival," and by the end of this classic he had broken into a grin. Robertson then shared the microphone with Danko for a simple and emotional rendition of "The Weight," backed by a couple-hundred-voice choir of fans, who sang along to the famed song. Toronto guitarist Colin Linden, along with his band, was lucky to be backing up these musical heroes.

"He got up there and this guitar tone came out of the amp, which was the tone that I had wanted to emulate my whole life — it was the greatest thing I had ever heard coming out of the amp next to me," Linden recalls. "It was really exciting." Following the gig, he says he was delirious with excitement: "I wanted to savour the moment forever. The important thing is that it was done with respect for the music. This wasn't an orchestrated happening; we specifically didn't want Robbie to feel pressure that he had to play. I'll never forget this."

That moment is one that still brings joy to Sprackman and makes him smile each and every time he recalls it. Like Linden, it's one he'll never forget. For him, The Band reuniting on the Horseshoe stage meant more — and was a bigger event — than any other surprise gigs that occurred years

(Above) Canadian music legend Robbie Robertson surprised everyone when he joined Colin Linden and The Band members Rick Danko and Garth Hudson onstage at the Horseshoe on March 13, 1989.

(Right) Rick Danko of The Band (*left*) performs with Colin Linden during one of the most memorable nights at the Horseshoe, on March 13, 1989.

later, including when the Rolling Stones played his bar in 1997. "There was Canadian music royalty all standing on my stage," Sprackman says. "They were all laughing and smiling. Whether they chatted beforehand, I don't know, but for me, and everyone who was in the Horseshoe that night, it was the surprise of a lifetime. I went to the bar and got a tray of B-52s, and for the next hour I walked around with trays of shooters on the house, getting everyone plastered."

* * *

Over the years, the Stones have had both love-ins and run-ins with the city of Toronto. From surprise gigs to arrests, there's no shortage of Stones stories about their visits to the Big Smoke. Gary LeDrew, who owned a speakeasy across the street from the Horseshoe Tavern in the 1970s, recalls the night when Mick Jagger called him up and came down to party long into the night. The band had also played a pair of intimate club gigs in town before. First in 1977, when they packed the tiny El Mocambo, and then in 1993, when they announced a surprise gig the day of the performance at the former RPM nightclub.

After reading about all the idols and icons from various genres of music who have played the Horseshoe stage since it opened in 1947 — from Willie and Waylon to the Police and Foo Fighters — it feels right that the self-proclaimed "world's greatest rock 'n' roll band" had to eventually play the legendary tavern.

The historic night happened on September 4, 1997, when the Stones were in town rehearsing at the Concert Hall for a tour that was to kick off at Soldier Field in Chicago later that month. The Stones were slated to appear later that night on the MTV Awards in New York City via satellite. Most people figured a TV crew would beam footage of the band live from their rehearsal space at Davenport and Yonge. But band sources confirmed that they wanted a barroom atmosphere in the background. And is there a better bar for the Rolling Stones to hold court in than the Horseshoe Tavern?

Even though the gig was to be kept secret, rumours spread faster than melted butter on toast. Block-long lines starting forming at 6:00 p.m., four hours before the band hit the stage. People crammed into the venue's front bar, hoping to get one step closer to seeing Mick, Keith, and the boys.

What many fans don't know is that the surprise gig almost never happened. Not everyone was thrilled with the Stones' secret show. Even though it was an honour for them to play in his bar, co-owner Kenny Sprackman minces no words when describing the whole affair: "It was a clusterfuck — a disaster. The rails had come up off the train track. The show was mishandled … it was a scary night. I didn't get to enjoy it at all."

The whole summer leading up to the secret gig, Sprackman says they had had a hard time closing the bar and getting people out every night, and it didn't matter what band was playing. The rumours of the Stones showing up and playing at the 'Shoe circulated for months beforehand. Then, when they finally did play, the Horseshoe's owners were some of the last people to find out about it. "We didn't know until forty-eight hours before the show," says Sprackman. "They told us, 'The Rolling Stones are going to play. Fill the club for us.'"

Security was out of control, according to Sprackman. "There were guard dogs everywhere, and actor John Goodman was drunk out of his tree working behind the bar," he adds. "Dan Aykroyd thought he was the tavern's new doorman, greeting everyone on Queen Street; he even threw out one of our employees!"

Bazil Donovan, bassist for Blue Rodeo, who had been a regular at the bar long before his band played there, was one of the lucky fans who made it in that September night. He almost didn't go. He certainly didn't know it was happening until less than an hour before the band hit the stage. Bazil lived farther west on Queen Street, near Parkdale. Many nights, if he didn't have a gig somewhere else, or wasn't on tour with Blue Rodeo, there was a good chance you would find him hanging out and listening to whoever was playing at the Horseshoe. You could call it his local to this day (even though he doesn't drink anymore). Despite having an ear to the inside, even he didn't know the gig was happening until he strolled down Queen Street and saw the crazy crowds. He shares the story of how that night played out:

> I had just come home from a session, and I was kind of tired.
> I thought, *Maybe I'll just stay in tonight.* I knew the Stones
> were in town, and I had been to a couple of parties where
> they were supposed to be and some of the band members
> like bassist Darryl Jones and the backup singers showed up.
> I was good friends with Dan Aykroyd and Richard Kruk …

but nobody told me they were playing. On the bill was a guy named Jack Ingram, a singer-songwriter from Texas. The only thing I knew about Jack Ingram was that Steve Earle had produced his album. Being a music lover, I figured if Steve Earle had produced him, this guy was pretty good.... I turned on the tube and there was nothing on, so I told myself to just go to the show and I would get my second wind. I walked to the corner of Spadina and [saw] a thousand people standing in front of the Horseshoe. I thought, *Jack Ingram is not that popular. What is going on?*

I went around to the back alley and the bouncer, Tyrone, told me the Stones were playing. I found Richard [Kruk] and said, "You have to let me in."

Richard talked to Aykroyd, who looked at me and at all these cops standing there, then said, "Bazil, come with me." He walks me in, and then tells me to go right to the middle and stay there. "You don't have a badge, so you will get kicked out if they catch you." I went to the middle of the room as instructed and stood there, and twenty minutes later the Stones came on. I remember always talking to people, if you could pick a band you could see in a bar it would be the Stones because their music so much lent [itself] to bars. I saw the show at RPM. I had been lucky enough to find out about that. But to see them at the Horseshoe, my local bar, and where I had played on that stage hundreds of times?

Jack Ingram was there, and he watched the show. Then everybody left and Jack played. By midnight, there was no sign the Rolling Stones had ever been there. Jack set up and did an hour set with his band. He joked, "Well, at least I've got a great story to tell when I get back to Texas: the night the Stones opened for me!"

Ingram, twenty-six years old at the time, was in Toronto as part of a mini tour promoting *Living or Dying* — a record he had made with Steve Earle and Ray Kennedy. Nearly twenty years on, the Lone Star State songwriter still recalls every minute of that magical day and milestone gig at the Horseshoe. They had pulled in to Hogtown in the early afternoon. As Ingram and his bandmates piled out of their tour van, one of the Horseshoe's owners greeted them and said not to worry, that the gig was still on:

> He doesn't tell us what is going on exactly, but says, "Everything is going to stay the same." We are like, "What are you talking about? Did we do something wrong?" He then explains the situation about the MTV Music Awards and the Stones playing an unannounced show before our set. The band and I say, "Okay, cool!" Then, we got everything ready. After, we just sat there in the back bar, which was completely empty. We just sat and waited for everyone to come. Everyone knew what was happening with the awards, but nobody knew they were also going to do a show. As soon as they were done, they hopped on stage. Everyone came rushing over. You couldn't move, and we didn't want to. In the middle of the Stones' set, my drummer and guitar player both had to take a leak, and they found bottles on the floor and peed in the bottles.
>
> I was right in the front row between Keith [Richards] and Mick [Jagger]. They got up and starting playing, and I distinctively remember Keith coming to the front of the stage doing a solo, leaning over and sweat landing on my face. He was that close! It was just unbelievable.
>
> As soon as they got offstage, the roadies moved their gear and I jumped onstage, grabbed my guitar, and we started playing.
>
> It was always funny to me, although I could never say it with a straight face, because it was so stupid, but everyone was always like, "The Rolling Stones opened for you!" Well, I guess technically, yes, they did. I remember the pressure. That experience alone was cool, but I wasn't there for the Stones; I was there to promote my record and get my career happening. I wasn't nervous, but I told my band before our set that we had to come out and every song had to totally rock, no

ballads. We started off with "Dim Lights, Thick Smoke," and we played every barroom brawl song we had. People stuck around; it was a killer night. That place probably packed in 500. If there were 500 people, by the time we stopped playing at midnight there were still 250 to 300 people in the bar.

An aside: My drummer didn't drink at the time; still he will tell you he doesn't drink, but [that's] a bit of a lie. We are used to 3.2 percent beer, at the most 5 percent; all the beer in Canada is 8 to 10 percent. It was right when Mike's Hard Lemonade came out. I remember only because my drummer hated beer, but he wanted to drink. We were all pretty hammered — wanted to drink, but not beer. He started to drink Mike's Hard Lemonade. At the end of the night we were going back to the hotel and he was talking to me really loud. I was thinking, "Either he doesn't understand how to drink, or he is having a stroke." Finally, he says, "I guess you may have noticed I had a few of the Mike's Hard Lemonade." It was a fun night!

Never met the Stones. That was another thing that hit me. It was amazing to me what a ballet they had going as far as how they were handled, how they were walked, it was a military operation. No, I did not meet Keith or Mick. They came in right when the camera said go.... Lights go off, five seconds later they are onstage, then when they finished their last song, five seconds later the stage was empty. It was insane and cool as hell. I remember they came in with their own monitors. Around our monitors, two wedges for [the] bass player, two wedges for [the] singer, two wedges for [the] guitar player ... [but] they had like fifteen to twenty wedges all across the front of the stage. It was amazing. It was so they could go all over the stage and never not know what was going on.

I also remember their clothes for some reason. Mick had on a green short-sleeve soft cotton shirt, button-down, open. Amazing to be that close and see Keith with shirt unbuttoned. Then to see Mick, halfway through the first song — he loses the shirt in a dramatic way. This is a show.

These motherfuckers are tight! It was cool as hell. As a performer, especially in our era and back then, the late nineties, it was shoe-gazer heaven. Everybody from that era, like Jeff Tweedy was looking at the floor; Jay Farrar never said a word to the audience. It was cool to pretend like you didn't give a shit. I remember always thinking, *I can't do that; I can't pretend like I don't care. I care too much.*

I was always like, *I'm going to go out there and entertain these guys into submission.* To see Mick Jagger and Keith Richards go out there as the heroes of all the shoe-gazers and put on a fucking show, I was like, *Aha! I knew it! I knew these motherfuckers weren't just dialling it in. I'm right.*

All that stuff was in my peripheral. John Goodman [was] there, Dan Aykroyd … there was a lot going on.… In hindsight, everything feels like you are watching it on the news or in retrospective, in slow motion, you can pick apart every part, but for me it was like, one, two, done, hotel. It was fucking quick! I do remember thinking at the time, *Wow, I'm a part of this evening, not just a bystander. No matter what my role is, I'm part of something way bigger than anything we [have] done before.*

"Brown Sugar" — I really remember that. The greatest part for me [was] getting in front of the stage. A lot of people never get to experience this part. They go to shows, but they've never dug their way to the front and been enveloped by the act. It's almost the same concept for me as putting on your headphones and reading the liner notes as the song is playing. You become a part of it; you get inside of it and are looking at it from the inside of the fish bowl. I do remember during "Brown Sugar" I was so busy watching the background singers and the bass player, Darryl Jones. I'll never forget watching. Every time I had seen the Stones on TV, or even in a big stadium, you focus on Mick, Keith, and sometimes Ronnie — you focus on the Rolling Stones. When I was in that moment, and they were playing "Brown Sugar," and there were all these intricate background parts, the … lady singers are killing it, and Darryl Jones is killing it, and he's doing all these rock moves right next to Keith, and all of a sudden I realize he's not a fill-in! It was like being inside an NFL football game or an NBA game where you are seeing the sweat, and how big these guys are, and how hard they are working, and what they are putting into it. It's that visceral thing where you just want to punch somebody because you are so amped up. I remember because of that song the way they were singing. Best musical memory of that night. That and just watching Keith, and when Keith Richards's sweat hit me! Not just in a fan kind of way, but more, *I'm part of this night!*

It was screaming loud. Because it was so loud, [I thought,] *If we come on and there is a dip in the volume, we will be fucked.* I went back and turned all of our monitors up to eleven. *We are going to play loud and fast!* Being the kind of touring act I am and have been since the beginning, versatility and elasticity is the only real fucking talent you need! Give it in a way that is above the fray to get noticed. Something I noticed early on that has helped over the years.

You don't have to shoot seventy in seventy degrees, no wind. All of a sudden you need to shoot sixty-eight in thirty-mile-per-hour gusts and it's raining. Like the way music is … success has afforded me a lot of changes. In general, I still have to be ready to do way better than head-liners under worse conditions. Even with number ones and top records, [I] still need to slug.

I knew it wasn't just a throwaway club. Like the Belly Up, I knew [the] Horseshoe was one of the great clubs of North America.

For those few hundred people who got in to the show, it was a surreal experience. Even though they were set to tour their new record, *Bridges to Babylon,* the forty-five-minute, twelve-song secret show leaned more heavily on Stones classics such as "Honky Tonk Women," "Under My Thumb," "19th Nervous Breakdown," and "Miss You."

The crowd went berserk when Richards struck the opening chords to "Start Me Up," and later drowned out Jagger during the chorus. They sang along to each word of hits like "Jumpin' Jack Flash" and the lone encore "Brown Sugar." The band even played a raucous, unbridled cover of Chuck Berry's classic "Little Queenie." According to the *Toronto Star*, singer Mick Jagger thanked the city for its hospitality, saying, "We've been very well treated here in Toronto. Everyone's been really, really good to us."

While The Band's onstage reunion was the *pièce de résistance* for his co-owner Sprackman, for X-Ray MacRae, the night the Stones rolled into the 'Shoe is definitely one of the most memorable of his nights spent in the iconic tavern:

> The Rolling Stones was a big night. All of a sudden I'm dealing with the biggest band in the world. I figured I should just put on a shirt of armour because I'm going to get shit thrown at me all night, but it was the easiest gig I did. They were so professional. They hung out in the office from 2:00 p.m. until they went on at 10:00. I had hung out with Keith before, but we won't get into those stories. He's just another guitar player. That's what he is. He would like to be invisible so he can play all the time. The lineups to try to get in were all the way down to the Black Bull. At 10:30 p.m. the night before, I was at a concert at the Molson Amphitheatre and my pager went off. It said: *X-Ray we want to have a surprise birthday party for a friend of mine and we want to have it at the Horseshoe tomorrow night. Meet me there at 2:30.*
>
> Here's the deal: the Stones' people told me, "If we hear anything about this before noon on the day of the show, it's cancelled." I didn't tell anyone except my brother in Kingston. I called him at 3:00 a.m. I didn't want to lose that gig. Are you crazy? No way. Lucky for me, it didn't leak out. It was a great night to see how professional bands like that are. Can you get a band any bigger? I don't think so.
>
> Mick and Keith had a bit of an argument. I wanted them to use our monitors, and Mick wanted to use their own, but they were too big for the Horseshoe. In the second

song, they had to turn their monitors off. They played with basically our house monitors after that, and they were fine. I walked into the dressing room. They were going on at nine o'clock, and I walked in about half an hour before they were set to go on. Somebody in the room said, "What are you going to play tonight?" They didn't have their set list together yet and they asked me, "What do you think we should do?" and I said, "'Little Queenie' — that is one of my favourite all-time songs." What do you know? They started out with that Chuck Berry tune.

Bartender Teddy Fury — who has been serving drinks at the Horseshoe coming on three decades now — agrees with MacRae that the Stones' show was one of the highlights of his tenure behind the 'Shoe's bar.

That was awesome. They played on a Thursday night. Two or three nights before, guys were coming in and checking out our PA system and talking to our soundman. You figured something was up. On the Wednesday night, we found out at midnight. They told X-Ray and Kenny, and said, "If anybody other than you two find out, we are pulling the gig and moving it somewhere else." I'm one of those people who can keep a secret. They were shitting their pants and had to tell somebody, so finally they let me know: "Teddy, don't breathe a word of this to anybody, but we've got the Stones tomorrow." I was pissed off because Thursday is my night off, but they said, "You are working it now!" That was fantastic. That night I met Keith Richards and it was great.

In those days, the offices used to be downstairs, the upstairs rock 'n' roll room was bigger, so we had a big sticker on the door that said "Emerald City," so that room was always referred to as Emerald City. Kenny Sprackman says at one point, "Teddy, take a case of water down to Emerald City." I go down there, open the door, and back my way in, and I see this couple standing in the back. I say to myself, *Shit! I think that's Ronnie Wood and his wife.* I'm a big Faces fan. There was this little beat-up art deco couch that we had, and I see what I think is a pile of clothes lying on it; then I realize it's Keith — he looked like one of those Macy's Day Parade things that they let the air out of. So, I'm down there. In my life I had met Mick Jagger once before and met Charlie Watts, but Keith Richards was the man. I turned to Ronnie Wood and said, "Sorry, I work here, they just told me to bring a case of water to you guys, I have keys … just a second." Then, I look at Keith … lean in, said something stupid like "Thanks for all the great music," and he takes my hand, it feels like a paper bag with yarn in it, and says something I can't understand, then starts laughing and shakes my hand. It's like I'm meeting Santa and I'm five years old. I walk out, lock the door, go up the stairs, and think, *I just met Keith Richards. I talked to him, even though I don't know what he said.* To this day, you can probably have me hypnotized, given truth serum, and ask me, "What did he say?" and I won't know. I kind of like the fact that I don't know.

Sean Dean, from the Sadies, was working the back bar during the Stones show:

One morning, I get a call around 11:00 a.m. from Nora [Gibbs], the manager and accountant at the Horseshoe when X-Ray owned the bar. I'm hungover, and I've been up all night. Nora is frantic on the phone. "Sean," she says, "you've got to get over here and come in to work right now."

I said, "Nora, this is my day off; there's no way I'm coming in to work. I'm hungover. I haven't had any sleep. I just had a beer right now. So I'm in no shape to come in to work."

She replied, "You have to come in. Your job depends on it."

"C'mon," I said, "it's a fuckin' Thursday. There's no way my job depends on it."

Then she lets it slip, "The Stones are playing!"

With those four words heard, I told her I'd be there in five minutes, as I lived right around the corner. I couldn't believe what she told me. I had met many celebrities working the bar, so knew it was possible. I get there, and there is a line around the block. Security guards had blocked off the whole back corner. Usually, I can go in the back door. There are these MTV massive satellite trucks there, and bodyguards everywhere. I get in, grab my credentials, and then grab my keys to the beer fridge.

I'm walking around getting ready for the show. I was told it was going to be a short show because MTV is just filming for an awards segment, supposedly featuring the Stones at the corner of the bar. I'm walking downstairs, and there he is — Mick Jagger — sitting on a chair where the phone booth is downstairs, just sitting there talking to one of his assistants. I just walk past him like it's no big thing. Then I see Keith Richards just hanging out. I can't believe it … if you had told me when I was listening to the Rolling Stones back in grade school that I would see them that close up one day, I would have been, *No way*. It was better than the Pope, better than Santa Claus! They did their segment and presented the award via satellite, and then they played. There were celebrities everywhere. As soon as the Stones started, John Goodman went to the back bar and started doing my job! He was doing this whole shtick, working the bar with Teddy [Fury] … frantically bringing cases of beer back and forth and playing along as if he was the barback for a couple of songs. It was so funny. That was one of the most fun times I've ever had at the Horseshoe. It was insane. The Stones were incredible. Went through some hit tunes. I just remember thinking how tremolo loud Keith was … I didn't realize how gnarly and loud and wild and tremolo his sound was; it was just so loud. I distinctly remember thinking that this is what rock 'n' roll is about, and having those amplifiers piercing and being in front of what you are hearing. It was so reassuring to hear the tone from Keith and hearing it with the amplifiers on the stage; that was the big part that melted my heart. Chicks around me were bawling constantly, leaning with their faces in their hands and bawling. A few times I got misty-eyed, too.

*   *   *

Besides good service and great music, the one other thing you're likely to find at the Horseshoe on any given night is a celebrity sighting or two — from Hollywood A-list actors and directors to National Hockey League players to legendary musicians who may be in town playing a bigger venue but will stop in after the show. The legendary status of the bar brings them out. For years when Dan Aykroyd's friends Richard Kruk and X-Ray MacCrae were involved, he would tell all of his buddies in the industry that if they were ever in Toronto they had to visit the Horseshoe. Quentin Tarantino and Mira Sorvino once drank at the front bar. The bartenders had a comp system when it came to celebrities: drinks were on the house. Other sightings over the years include actor Rutger Hauer, Ray Davies of the Kinks, and Malcolm McLaren, the recording artist and fashion designer who was once the manager of the Sex Pistols.

"It's one of those places where on any given night of the week you would see people drop in," says Sean Dean. "If they were in town doing a movie, somehow the word would get out that the Horseshoe was the place to go. In the early Blue Rodeo days, I'll never forget it, we would look out and Tom Cruise would be there watching us play. One New Year's Eve, my cousin, who is a bit obnoxious, went over and kissed him, and he left right afterwards! He was shooting *Cocktail* in town, with Bryan Brown. He used to come and see us all the time, came to about five of our shows. The comedian Steven Wright also came to see us a lot in the early days."

*   *   *

September 19, 1996, signalled another memorable surprise show at the 'Shoe. This time it was the Canadian kid who just wants to rock: Bryan Adams. The Vancouver musician, in town for the MuchMusic Video

This kid just wants to rock. Bryan Adams plays a surprise gig at the 'Shoe on September 20, 1996.

Awards, decided to return to his roots of playing dives rather than stadiums by giving an impromptu concert. Following his duties at the awards show down the street, three hundred lucky fans packed into the Horseshoe for an unforgettable night of rock 'n' roll. Tickets for the show were offered on a rush basis for only twenty dollars. What made the show even more special was Adams's unlikely set list. As Peter Howell wrote in his review for the *Toronto Star*, "The mood of the evening was set from the opening song, a cover of Texas good ol' boy Lee Roy Parnell's raunchy 'If the House Is Rockin'.'" Rather than rolling out his own hits, the thirty-six-year-old mainly covered a variety of rock 'n' roll classics for the rest of the night: from the Beatles' "Twist and Shout" and the Kingsmen's "Louie Louie" to paying homage to fellow Canadian songwriters such as Tom Cochrane with "Life Is a Highway" and Bachman-Turner Overdrive with "Takin' Care of Business." Adams made sure to include a few of his mega hits, like "Summer of '69," to satisfy the fans. It all added up to another historic Horseshoe night that didn't end until nearly 2:00 a.m. As Howell wrote, "It was easily the best Adams show I've ever seen."

* * *

Like Bryan Adams, before moving on to bigger venues the Tragically Hip honed their Canadiana rock sound at clubs like the Horseshoe. From the 'Shoe's stage is where the charisma of lead singer Gord Downie caught the eyes and ears of Bruce Dickinson, president of MCA Records, who signed The Hip back in 1987, after seeing them play a gig there the previous year. Later, the band even immortalized the venue in their song "Bobcaygeon," in which Downie sings "That night in Toronto, / With its checkerboard floors" in reference to the 'Shoe's dance floor.

The Tragically Hip gave many surprise shows at the iconic Toronto bar over the years. Jake Gold, the band's manager, had a good relationship with the owners and loved to use the club as a place to launch albums and iron out the kinks before hitting the road and playing bigger arenas across the country. One of these many "surprise" shows occurred on April 18, 1992. The concert was not announced publicly; instead, the Bourbon Tabernacle Choir, on the tail end of a three-night stand, was listed as the headliner. But

Gord Downie of the Tragically Hip, taken in the dressing room of the Horseshoe Tavern.

for the Hipsters in the know, it wasn't hard to figure out that Gord Downie and his bandmates were scheduled to make an appearance. Word on the street travelled fast. The band took the stage at 11:30 p.m., following a set by the Bourbons, and borrowing their equipment. The evening was a showcase to preview The Hip's forthcoming third studio release, *Fully Completely*, before they hit the road for a two-week jaunt across Australia. The album went on to be the band's most commercially successful record, selling more than one million copies in Canada and achieving diamond status. *Toronto Star* critic Peter Howell described the evening as "a night for exploration and adventure for all concerned." Besides the new songs, The Hip offered up a couple of songs from *Road Apples* during the encore.

Long-time Horseshoe Tavern bartender Teddy Fury recalls many other gigs when The Hip played the Horseshoe — driving down in their van from their hometown of Kingston — sometimes mid-week to an audience of "nobody" in the early days, and then later, like the aforementioned surprise show, to sold-out crowds.

Flash forward twenty-four years: It's no surprise to learn that on August 20, 2016, the bar was one of many venues across the country to host a viewing party of The Hip's final concert, simulcast on television and radio from Kingston on CBC. Hundreds of fans crammed the back bar to say goodbye to one of Canada's most treasured bands of the past thirty years.

10

Tales from the Bar

Pissing off the bartender can be a sobering experience.
— Anonymous

A bartender is just a pharmacist with a limited inventory.
— Anonymous

NEXT TO A HANDS-ON CLUB OWNER, or maybe the doorperson, who knows more about a place than the one who serves the drinks? That's certainly the case at the Horseshoe Tavern, where there's a pair of bartenders who are almost as legendary as the place itself: Teddy Fury and Bob Maynard. This chapter is dedicated to them.

When Teddy and I meet at a Starbucks on a Tuesday night to talk about the Horseshoe Tavern, he's like a kid in an arcade who can't decide which game to play first; he jumps from one tale to another. Hours quickly pass. Starbucks closes, and we shuffle up the street to the place where all those magical moments happened. As he regales me with story after story from his twenty-nine years tending bar, he laughs every few minutes, remembering all the crazy nights and memorable days spent working and playing between the weathered old walls.

Where to begin? Well, at the beginning. Teddy started slinging drinks behind the Horseshoe's bar back in 1987. Before getting the gig, he had played there several times since 1977 with various rockabilly bands he was in, such as the Royal Crowns. He says his band was one of last ones to play there before the stage was moved from where the back bar is today to the north wall at the back of the room.

Teddy Fury, the man behind the bar for
more than three decades; his stories are
as legendary as the tavern.

Teddy's first time playing the 'Shoe was around 1977, when he was in
a band called the Bobcats, who opened for Willie English. "We sucked that
night!" he recalls, in his typical self-deprecating manner. "Wayne Gretzky
probably remembers missing the net more than he does putting it in!"

Years later, the fact that he had played in a bunch of bands there eventually led to him being offered the bartending gig. Teddy remembers:

> I got kicked out of a band and was a mess at the time.
> I didn't know what I was going to do. My playing had
> deteriorated. I knew X-Ray [MacRae] and I knew Kenny
> [Sprackman] since about 1977. Met Kenny first when he
> was running the Hotel Isabella. X-Ray was in Kingston,
> but had a used record store, Used Grooves, that I would
> always visit when my band played there. I recall going to
> his record store; he was a burly bear of a guy, a gentle giant.
> He totally dug rockabilly, and we hit it off, like Laurel and

Hardy. I met Kenny around the same time, and we always kept in touch. When I lost my job gigging, I had never been a bartender before, but they offered me the job. I was never Mr. Self-Confidence. I remember saying, "I don't think I can be a bartender," and they said, "We've seen you on the other side of the bar, and you are really good at that!" My joke is, nearly thirty years later, I'm still on my three-month trial, but I still don't have a nametag or a uniform!

Jokes aside, Fury certainly doesn't need a nametag. Having tended bar that long, he's a fixture, not just at the Horseshoe but also across the city. Everyone knows Teddy. When he started tending bar at the Horseshoe, a domestic bottle of beer cost $1.85. He says, over the years, the various ownership changes have always been an exercise in flux, but they've also been very organic and he's never had any issues with any of the owners. By the time Jeff Cohen came on board as an owner, Teddy had already gotten to know him, since he had been the talent buyer for a decade already. "What has been great about all the owners of the Horseshoe is that they like the people, and the vibe they create is not at all corporate … it's very family-oriented. Sure, we've all been suspended for stuff over the years, but they are very hands-off. A lot of times many of us feel like we are the owners, and when people ask us, we say, 'No, we just act like it.'"

Teddy says what makes the Horseshoe Tavern tick is that it doesn't have an identity crisis: it's a blue-collar bar today, and it always has been. "If people come in and ask for a mojito, I tell them we have a Moe Howard! I call it a meat-and-potatoes bar. We have Chardonnay and Chardon B!" While it may be a blue-collar bar, that doesn't mean there's any trouble. In his nearly thirty years there, he's seen only one fight.

Fury says they've figured out what works, and you can always expect the bookings to not suck. "That has been the consistent thing with the Horseshoe, even before I worked here, and I wasn't playing and I was a patron," says Teddy. "I would have a Friday night off, and come here knowing that whatever is on would be good. I could literally count on one hand the amount of bands that have sucked. There have been plenty that were mediocre, but in almost thirty years, there's been maybe five that shouldn't have been there."

*   *   *

Enough of the backstory. It's time for Teddy to share a few of his most memorable 'Shoe stories. Here's a quick one to start:

> When Kenny was still working here, the great thing was that he loved cars. One day, he had parked his car, some slick Jag, out front. We had just hired a busboy named Steve Richards. Kenny comes walking in and goes, "Jesus Christ, there is some 1950s white dump truck out back. Who the fuck owns that? Let's get it towed!" And I went, "Kenny, I want you to meet Steve; he's our new busboy. He owns the truck." Then, he goes, "That's fuckin' great!" Later, when the drivers for the Beer Store were on strike, they sent Steve in his dump truck to the brewers directly; he filled his whole dump truck with like three hundred cases of beer. It looked like the Mardi Gras Welfare Parade. It was so awesome; that's a total Horseshoe story.

Teddy remembers fondly the night when John Entwistle from The Who was in town:

> It was mid- to late February, on a Monday or Tuesday night. I was working the front bar. There was an independent record label in Hamilton at the time called Gritty City; they were doing a whole night with their bands. It ended up turning into one of those nights. We didn't have much snow that winter, and then all of a sudden at five o'clock, everything is iced over, then about 8:30 p.m. it got mild again. I was working with a guy named Chris Dignan, who was in the band Suckerpunch and later Dodge Fiasco. There was no one in the back, maybe fifteen people, but all the bands that were playing were great. Around 9:00 p.m. this couple comes in. A tall, thin guy in his mid-forties. The woman is pretty. They both have overcoats on. Me and Chris go, "Is that John Entwistle?" We weren't sure, but then he takes off

his coat and he has this giant gold spider on a chain. Think of his famed song "Boris the Spider." It was a total *Spinal Tap* moment. We said, "It's got to be him!"

Ever since Kenny and X-Ray owned the bar, we had a comp system, whereby you can comp a few drinks if you ever get someone in there and can keep them there. She orders a couple of drinks, and he's not saying much. I think they paid for the first couple of rounds; then, as the banter was loosening up, everyone figured out who it was, the place wasn't jammed, but he was kind of holding court. He was really great. He ended up drinking a bottle and a half of Rémy Martin. There were about five bands playing, and everyone would come and he'd say, "Show me your guitar," then he would point out all the fine points to them. He was fuckin' awesome. Guys asked for autographs, and he was happy to sign. He was hangin' out. By 2:00 a.m., he is our oldest pal in the world. His wife is going, "We are having our house renovated," and showing us pictures of their pad in Hollywood; then, John goes, "Listen, I don't think these boys are interested in that. I'll show you my guitar collection." And he had this photo album with him. At one point, I remember this, he is making requests. It was so effing great! Later, he said, "Do you want to know how to really piss off Roger Daltrey?" He gets a cigarette and blows smoke in our faces. He is telling us all these great stories. At one point, we just happened to have on "Pretty Woman," which I think anyone since the cavemen has played air guitar to. Chris is walking by, doing the air guitar riff, and Entwistle goes, "Chris," and plays it to him. It was just like something out of *Wayne's World*. He was the most accommodating, lovely guy. But the spider on the chain? It was like, *Are you kidding me?*

Teddy says he misses many of the regulars who used to hang out in the front bar:

The rounders. Now they were real characters. Look around in the bar today, and you'll see we have plaques up for some of the people who were regulars here. At one time there were all these knitting mills around the Horseshoe, which have been knocked down over the years and replaced with giant high-rises.

We had this one regular named Jimmy. He was a little guy, about my size, with a little moustache; he looked like Clark Gable. He drank Labatt Blue and was a killer pool player. The more drunk he got, the better he got. I remember one Christmas Eve, he was in and we had cut him off early, but he didn't want to leave. He was sitting there playing pool; he always had a Labatt Blue in one hand, a cigarette in the other, and his lighter across from him. He would always turn to me and go, "Teddy, give me another funny one!" He was fantastic!

There was another guy named Rudy who used to live at the Black Bull, across the street from Marty's Diner (where a Subway franchise lives now). Now Rudy, he was a girl man. Coming in one afternoon, I had just arrived, and he yells, "Here comes the little cocksucker that gets all that pussy!" How poetic is that? It's the best Charles Bukowski–like compliment I ever heard. I've told that story to my daughter!

There was one other guy, Danny, that we called Red. He sold those *Outreach* newspapers. He once wrote an IOU for a double Scotch on a napkin that we had up on the bar for about five years. He was awesome. He knew the streets. There is a horrible news story from 1977 that speaks to the end of the innocence in Toronto, when a twelve-year-old shoeshine boy named Emanuel Jaques got raped and murdered by some creepy guys down at the Zanzibar on Yonge Street. One day, I'm working and some creepy-looking older guys came into the Horseshoe. Danny said to me, "Teddy, do you remember Emanuel Jaques? Yea? Well, those were two of the guys that were in on it. Don't serve them!" I don't know how he knew, but we threw them out.

There's been many a night when Teddy and the rest of the staff closed down the bar with various bands that were playing elsewhere in town: from British rockers Oasis to Celtic rockers the Pogues. Besides the Rolling Stones' surprise show, when Teddy met Keith Richards (a story Teddy shares in detail in the preceding chapter), a few of his most memorable shows include Johnny Thunders doing two nights and Chris Isaak playing right around the time his hit "Wicked Game" came out: "I thought there would be about a hundred people, but ended up being about six hundred … it was just jammed."

And there was Chris Hillman, formerly of the Byrds, who played the 'Shoe one night with his Desert Rose Band. "They were on tour as an opening act for somebody. They played the 'Shoe on a night off for two and a half hours," Teddy remembers. "That is one of the greatest shows I've ever seen. All [the members of] that band [were] heavy players."

Teddy says there are probably another thousand bands that never went anywhere, "but on a given night the planets aligned and they were the kings of music that night." The one thing that sucks about bartending at a live music venue, he says, is that you don't really get to see the show when you're behind the bar: "If it's a two-night stand by a band, I like to come back the night I'm not working."

Is Teddy, going on thirty years at the bar, set to retire any time soon? He doesn't think so, as long as his passion for the people and the place is still there. "One time I was off work, and I thought what if I won the lottery, I wouldn't have to work at the Horseshoe again, but then I thought at the same time, if I had won, I would probably still come in anyway because I love it so much.

"Fellow bartender Bob [Maynard] and I joke that when we go we want to get taxidermied! We will be like automatons. Some people might say the service will be better!"

*   *   *

Bob Maynard has been bartending for thirty-one years — the bulk of them at the Horseshoe Tavern. He jokes this tenure is thirty-two and a half too many! Most likely, shortly after this book hits the shelves Bob will be retired, enjoying time at his Georgian Bay cottage, maybe moving out of Toronto to somewhere less expensive like Dundas or Hamilton, Ontario. So, how did he get the gig in the first place?

After working for Kenny Sprackman at the Hotel Isabella in the early 1980s, Bob worked out west for four years, where he had managed the biggest bar in Whistler. Coming back to Toronto, he had a hard time finding work since he was applying for bartending gigs and they felt he had too much experience. Then, by chance, he and his wife walked in to the Horseshoe one day looking for work. They were chatting with the bar's manager, and out came Sprackman from his office to offer Bob a job.

Unlike Teddy, Maynard is not a music guy. He's content to work the front bar, away from the instruments crashing and the sounds of whatever band is playing. "I'm not a musician, and I've always found the quieter spot the easier of the two bartending stations. The other reason: the people in the front room are there for one reason — to drink — so I know I'm going to make more money from the drinkers."

Unlike the back bar, which is usually packed with music lovers, the regulars Bob sees in the front at night are a mix of characters: from street people to Bay Street lawyers, stockbrokers, and retailers. In his thirty-one years, like Teddy, Bob's seen little trouble. He's had to drag a few people outside, but that's about it. Everyone in the front bar usually gets along. It's a bit like the 1980s sitcom *Cheers* — where everybody knows your name. "It still bewilders me sometimes how seldom there are confrontations," says Maynard. "It's just the tone of the place … it just never gets ugly. It's a blue-collar bar where nobody has any pretence. It's just, 'This is who I am, and I'm here to have a good time.'"

After the bar closes, or during special occasions like one of the other bartenders' birthdays, the staff at the Horseshoe Tavern can get up to some hijinks. Bob recalls one of these celebrations: "Four of us got up on stage wearing nothing but the Horseshoe underwear we sell at the front bar. We put it on backward, though, so the horseshoe was on our butts!" Bob says all the staff members at the 'Shoe like to have fun. At heart, they are just a bunch of "goofs."

Beyond the tips, one wonders what's kept Bob there for three decades. "The tits!" he says, laughing. "Even my wife would tell you that. Over the years, I've seen lots of big tits."

During his tenure there Maynard says he's thought about calling it quits a few times, but life circumstances prevented him from pulling the plug on the Horseshoe gig. Generally, it's an easy room to work and the money is good. It's allowed him to buy a house and put his kids through college. One change he isn't as thrilled about is how they must now be polite to everyone, even customers who are not nice. "Back in the day, we were given more freedom in how we were allowed to deal with customers," he says. "Kenny's philosophy was the customer is always wrong, so we did not have to put up with any nonsense. If someone was being a jerk, you get what you give. We were allowed to express our opinions. Now, we are supposed to say yes, sir, or no, sir."

Bob's shift in the front bar usually begins at 7:00 p.m. He hasn't worked during the day in twenty-five years. He sees a changing clientele. There used to be sixty or seventy people every night. All of them played pool, and they all knew each other. "It was a unique atmosphere," Maynard says. "We don't get the after-work crowd we used to. People are more conscious about drinking and driving, and lots of businesses have relocated from downtown to the suburbs, places like Scarborough and Vaughan."

When Bob started pouring drinks at the Horseshoe, they didn't have doormen. You didn't need them. You did not need to worry for your safety because the other staff and your fellow customers would police things. "That doesn't exist anymore," he says.

Last fall, Maynard received a one-hundred-dollar tip on two beers. The patron had already had two or three rounds. "After he had bought two beers, he gave me $120 and said give me change for twenty. I wanted to give it back, but his friend goes, 'Keep it. He can afford it, and he's having fun. You were funny with us and we're having a good time, so Merry Christmas!'"

11

Ushering In a New Era

Change is inevitable. Change is constant.
— Benjamin Disraeli

CHANGE CAME TO THE HORSESHOE again around 1995, when Jeff Cohen, known by most as simply J.C., and his partner Craig Laskey arrived at the 'Shoe. They were invited by Sprackman to usher in the modern era for the storied tavern. If the shoe fits, wear it. And that's exactly what Cohen did when he arrived at the Horseshoe. He knew the venue needed to change its course. That was a given. What wasn't so clear, at first, was what direction he and his partner Laskey would take it in.

* * *

Jeff Cohen was born and raised in Montreal. After high school, he moved to Ottawa to attend Carleton University. It was only two hours away from home, and he could get there easily by car, bus, or train. "That's where I first gained my independence," Cohen says.

While in the nation's capital, Cohen spent more time at the campus radio station, CKCU FM, than in the classroom. That's where his real education happened, and eventually he dropped out of school to work full-time at the station. From 1981 to 1991, he worked as a DJ, doing sports and public affairs and playing punk rock music. He laughs when he tells me the only reason he remembers the year he started there was because that was the first and only time his beloved Montreal Expos made the post-season.

"I was a muzoid," recalls Cohen. "That era was the right time, as it saw one of the greatest explosions in rock 'n' roll. I learned more in a three-minute record than I ever learned in school. I failed three times, and eventually Carleton kicked me out."

As luck would have it, Cohen was surrounded by a lot of young, bright minds at the station, many of whom would go on to great success in the music industry. The program director at CKCU was Nadine Gelineau. After leaving the campus radio station, she would go on to work for BMG Canada and later start a North America–wide music marketing and branding agency called the MuseBox. Sadly, she passed away in April 2016. Another colleague, John Westhaver, now runs the biggest independent music store in Ottawa: Birdman Sound. "There was a bit of an incubator going on," Cohen says. "I fell into that scene."

Later, as Cohen was forging his own path in the music industry — a long, winding road that eventually led him to the hallowed space at 370 Queen Street West — he relied on many of these early mentors he met while working at CKCU.

While at the station, Cohen took on a series of successive roles that kept building the skills he would need the day he took over the 'Shoe. First, he became the fundraising director for the non-profit station. One way he achieved this was by putting on CKCU-sponsored concerts. Bands he booked included Rheostatics, U.I.C., the Gruesomes, Fugazi, Ministry, Circle Jerks, the Dead Milkmen, and Henry Rollins. Mostly, these were bands with a punk rock attitude. He made the station money, and he says that's where he first learned to become a promoter. Later, he started an all-ages club called One Step Beyond that hosted a lot of live music. After two years, the venture failed. It was time to try something new.

Out of work and in love, Cohen moved to Toronto to chase a girl. Unfortunately, she wasn't as interested and never went out with him again. It was around September 1992. Cohen arrived in the big city adrift and alone. He had no sense of what he was going to do next. He only knew three people in town: Dave "Bookie" Bookman, whom he had met through his band the Bookmans when they had played in Ottawa; Elliott Lefko, a Toronto promoter who went on to become a big talent buyer across North America; and Fred Robinson, from the punk band U.I.C. None of them had any association with the Horseshoe Tavern.

The Smugglers, from Vancouver, pictured here in the basement dressing room prior to their gig at the Horseshoe on February 12, 2000.

Cohen decided to start by tapping in to his decade of experience at the community radio station in Ottawa. He approached CIUT (89.5 FM), the campus station for the University of Toronto, and got on the air as a volunteer, hosting an overnight show. With his ten years of radio experience, it wasn't long before the station gave him his own show called *Mods and Rockers*, which featured punk, ska, and mod music.

Within six months of landing in Toronto, however, Jeff still didn't have a full-time job. He wasn't yet promoting any shows, as it appeared there were already enough promoters in town. But when he wasn't on air, he started to make the rounds and schmooze with the doormen and managers at all the live music venues that mattered: the Rivoli, the Diamond Club (now the Phoenix), and the Horseshoe.

At the same time, his *Mods and Rockers* show took off. Elliott Lefko liked his show, and his buddy Bookman, who was a broadcaster at CFNY (102.1 The Edge), started introducing him to other people in Toronto's music scene. At some point during that time, Cohen remembers receiving a phone call from William New, lead singer of Groovy Religion and the head bartender at the Apocalypse Club, and the inventor of Elvis Mondays. He said to Cohen, "Elliott used to be the talent buyer at the Apocalypse, but he left. I've taken over, and I'm losing money at the bar because I can't book it that well. Have you ever done this before?"

Cohen says he thought, *I've fundraised for a radio station, I can do this.* A deal was soon reached for Cohen to come on board at New's club for a three-month trial. Like that, he had his first paying job in Toronto. For the next few years, that's where he cut his teeth and continued to build up his reputation among the rest of the industry players. It's not clear whether Sprackman was watching Cohen at this stage, but it wouldn't be too long before he learned about his future partner and the person who would be the perfect fit to take the Horseshoe Tavern into the new century.

At the Apocalypse, Cohen was booking mostly punk and garage rock bands. Later, he dabbled a bit in speed metal. There were some memorable shows there, including a double bill featuring two bands from the United Kingdom, Snuff and Bad Manners. For most of us, as we age, our musical tastes evolve. Cohen, just entering his thirties, started to dig the blues. Albert's Hall, the top floor of the Brunswick House on Bloor Street, was the venue at the time. They brought in some legendary performers for week-long residencies. As his path of musical discovery continued, he learned more about offshoots of the genre, like zydeco and soul. Somehow, through this journey, he became friends with the Bourbon Tabernacle Choir, a rhythm and blues and funk fusion alternative band formed in 1985. By the early 1990s, they were holding court on campus radio. "They are one of the greatest Canadian bands that ever existed, regardless of how far they went or didn't go," says Cohen. "They are one of greatest live bands I have ever seen. They were all ex–punk rockers who got into soul and the blues. I started hanging out with them a lot, especially Chris [Brown]."

Eventually, around 1994, Cohen became a consultant for the Bourbons. Through them, he got introduced to their accountant, Lawrence Sprackman, Kenny Sprackman's brother. One of the final pieces of the puzzle that led him to the Horseshoe was then in place. After three years, Cohen quit the Apocalypse Club and started to promote his own shows at various venues around town.

Work at the Mariposa Folk Festival, at the El Mo as a booking agent and club talent buyer, and for the Agency as an agent for a brief stint, followed. Heck, Cohen figured an agent was one of the few jobs he hadn't done yet in the business, so he rolled the dice. That's where he first became friends with Ralph James, who today is the biggest talent agent in Canada. "I remember him asking me, 'If you were an agent, who would you sign?'" Cohen recalls. "I told him: 'Lowest of the Low, Big Sugar, and Rheostatics.'"

Although the Horseshoe wasn't his room to book (that was James's territory), Cohen was assigned the Ultrasound and he went on to sign the likes of 13 Engines, Rheostatics, Big Sugar, Lowest of the Low, Big Rude Jake, and Monster Voodoo Machine for that stage. But when Sam Feldman, of the biggest artist management group in western Canada, acquired the Agency, Cohen was let go.

So it was back to the El Mocambo, where Cohen had spent some time earlier in the decade. The club had just reopened yet again with new owners. At that time, Cohen had signed a band named Bender, managed by a guy named Craig Laskey. The two got along, and Cohen asked Laskey to be his assistant. This new partnership lasted for a year at the El Mo before they were fired for not sharing the same direction as the owners. The two remained partners and brainstormed about what would come next.

The Sadies during one of their annual New Year's Eve performances at the 'Shoe on December 31, 2006.

They had been out of work for only a couple of weeks when Cohen got a call from Lawrence Sprackman asking if he would consider working for his brother Kenny over at the Horseshoe. Bookie, who knew Jeff from their Ottawa days, had also put in a good word with Kenny. "He's at his wits end," Lawrence said of his brother's predicament. "The Horseshoe is not doing well, and he needs help."

Yvonne Matsell had decided to go back to the Ultrasound full-time, so Kenny Sprackman was desperate for a new talent buyer for the club, someone who had their pulse on the current music scene. Craig and Jeff conferred on the matter and felt the 'Shoe was out of their league. At the El Mo, they booked music three, maybe four nights a week, whereas the 'Shoe was a seven-nights-a-week bar. "At the time, we were managing both 13 Engines and Big Rude Jake and thought maybe we will just go into management full-time," Cohen says. "The accountant understood our trepidation, but asked if we could do him a favour and just meet with his brother."

The band Wilco was doing sound check when Cohen and Laskey arrived for their interview with Kenny Sprackman. X-Ray was not there. "Craig was more freaked out about meeting Jeff Tweedy [Wilco's lead singer] than about the interview," Cohen says, laughing. "It was the strangest interview I've ever had in my life. He [Kenny] wasn't someone who looked through your resumé. I gave it to him, and he just threw it in the corner. 'Don't you have any questions to ask?' I said. Kenny just looked at Craig and [me] and said, 'I've heard great things from my brother. When can you guys start? Let's set a figure, and we're done.'"

To put this bold offer into context, this was after the club's heyday in the late 1980s and early to mid-1990s. They had weathered the recent recession, but once again, the club was trying to find its musical mojo. "Please help me. This place is an institution," Kenny pleaded with the pair. Sprackman really hoped the answer to his booking problems lay in these two young musical minds sitting across from him.

Cohen recalls leaving that meeting and telling Kenny his proposition was overwhelming. "We want to do the talent buying, but we need some time to decide."

It took Jeff and Craig about a month to decide. They put together a plan for the changes they needed to make. At the time, the 'Shoe was a place that wasn't welcoming to every promoter in town. "We had this vision to make it more open and bring in more Canadian bands," says Cohen.

Andy Maize, lead singer for the Skydiggers, playing at one of the band's annual Christmas shows, December 19, 2008.

They would also require some start-up money to implement some of the changes. "For one, there was no advance ticketing in the place," Cohen adds. "There was not a lot of professionalism in the room, either, as they didn't have their own sound technician. Kenny gave us carte blanche. 'Just tell me what you need, and it's yours,'" Cohen says they were told.

On August 1, 1995, Cohen and Laskey took over the day-to-day booking and talent buying for the club.

* * *

Laskey grew up in Port Perry, Ontario. From an early age, music caught his ear. He listened late into the night to the radio waves in his bedroom and started getting fascinated with the live music scene as a teen. "I would go to Toronto by myself and see whoever was playing at Maple Leaf Gardens or the CNE," he recalls.

Following high school, Laskey attended Durham College, taking the arts and business entertainment program with the dream of working in the live music industry. On the side, he also started managing a few local bands.

After finishing his diploma, he started managing Bender, a band from Orangeville, which Cohen ended up booking; that's when the pair first met and started a friendship based on a shared love of music. This burgeoning friendship led to Cohen bringing Laskey on board to book bands at the El Mocambo and, later, at the Horseshoe. Asked to recall some of the favourite gigs he's brought to the 'Shoe, the booking agent mentions a handful: Wilco, the Baseball Project (three-fifths of R.E.M.), the Pixies, Link Ray, the Dead Weather with Jack White, Son Volt on a Sunday night, the Strokes' second-ever Toronto show on a Nu Music Tuesday, Guided by Voices for two nights in 2002, and, of course, all the last-minute Tragically Hip shows. "It's hard to put into words, but I still get a lot of joy booking the club six nights a week," Laskey says. "For some bands, it's a milestone for them just to play the Horseshoe, even if they don't go on to major fame. It's special to think I'm a part of that." Cohen remembers:

> When Craig and I came in as talent buyers at the Horseshoe, we worked alongside X-Ray for the first few years. He still had a lot of passion for the music, and we valued his opinion, even though his tastes were not up to speed with what the kids were now listening to. There was no animosity between the three of us. We told him, we want to be like you, but do our own thing. We asked him what he was listening to and tried our best to keep him involved. He really helped us. We picked his mind and sat and listened to music with him in his basement office, which was filled floor to ceiling with cassette tapes.

By the end of that first year, thanks to the pair's booking policies, they had improved the back bar sales by one hundred thousand dollars. Certain staff didn't like the changes, which also included signing a deal with Ticketmaster, building the stage a little higher, putting the door staff under Cohen and Laskey's control (not the owners'), and getting rid of one of the house technicians. They replaced a few staff — realizing they needed personnel in the back bar who knew music. They also kicked out a whole bunch of bands who were used to playing there and getting steady gigs — local favourites like

Bazil Donovan, bassist for Blue Rodeo, performs as part of the Six Shooter Records Outlaws & Gunslingers Americana Music Association Showcase at Canadian Music Fest on March 20, 2013.

Jack de Keyzer and Paul James. Cohen said it wasn't personal. They were great bands, but their time had passed its prime. "We needed to give new bands like Big Sugar, the Mahones, and Great Big Sea a chance to play here."

Jeff and Craig brought in some surf and rockabilly bands from the States — stuff X-Ray dug like Dick Dale. They also started paying homage to some unheralded artists from the sixties and seventies like Jimmie Dale Gilmore. "All the while, we were adding our own touch," says Cohen. "Kenny let us do our thing. We really got that place rocking! At the end of the first year, he asked us to sign on for another two years."

The pair was having fun, so signing another deal was a non-issue. Their reputation was building, especially among agents like Ralph James, for whom Jeff had previously worked at the Agency. The whole key to the Horseshoe, even when X-Ray was booking it, was that James always had these incredible bands to offer the venue. Somewhere along the line, what happened was that for some reason the 'Shoe was not booking in as many of James's bands. "He was the one signing a lot of the bands that were a perfect fit for the 'Shoe, so when I took over I also re-established the Ralph James era," Cohen says. "He built bands' careers off that stage."

Miranda Mulholland is all smiles and fiddling about on the Horseshoe stage as part of NXNE 2014 Outlaws & Gunslingers Six Shooter Records showcase, June 19, 2014.

Starting in 1997, Laskey and Cohen started an annual pilgrimage, often joined by X-Ray, to the South by Southwest (SXSW) music festival in Austin, Texas, scouting out new bands to bring north of the border to the Horseshoe. It was there where they discovered many of the alt-country bands for the first time that they would soon book, such as Ryan Adams, the Old 97's, and Neko Case. The trio hung out, and X-Ray showed them all his favourite spots, including the best place for barbecue: the Green Mesquite. More than twenty years on, Craig and Jeff throw a party at the restaurant every year in honour of X-Ray.

* * *

"We made [the Horseshoe] a place people felt comfortable to go to," explains Cohen. "Elliott [Lefko] from MCA Concerts started putting all of his shows into the Horseshoe. We also had deep connections with Dave Bookman and Kim Hughes at CFNY, and we changed the structure of Dave's Nu Music Night and it exploded."

On Bookie's Tuesday night, the Horseshoe started doing crazy bands like Son Volt, Whiskeytown, the Jayhawks, the Strokes, Goldfinger, and even Foo Fighters. "Everything just clicked," recalls Cohen. "Our methodology worked for the 'Shoe, and the 'Shoe worked for us."

The other thing that's key to the more recent success of the Horseshoe is the creation and establishment of associations and partnerships with music media such as *Chart* magazine, *Exclaim!*, and *NOW Magazine*, and with record labels like Six Shooter Records and Dine Alone Records, along with the independent record stores in town that sell tickets to the shows. "We told all of them, we want a relationship with you," explains Cohen. "We are all small businesses and in this together."

Cohen and Laskey initially had opposition from some employees and external partners who didn't like change. The bar manager in charge gave them a hard time when they first assumed control. And a few publicists and promoters didn't like the direction they were taking the bar. The reality is that they didn't like it because it wasn't friendly to the bands they were promoting. "Some just wanted it to be the way it was ten years ago," Cohen says. "Some were just not interested in our new vision. They felt that we were straying from the roots music stuff that was at the core of the 'Shoe's legacy. We didn't care."

Instead, thanks to Laskey's ear and ability to hear a hot band before anyone else, they brought in the likes of Neutral Milk Hotel, Death Cab for Cutie, and The National. Many of the bands they booked were playing Massey Hall or the Air Canada Centre the next time they returned to town. All of them started at the 'Shoe, playing for five hundred bucks. Rheostatics, whom Cohen got to know when they were doing two-week stands at Ultrasound, were convinced to come and do the same length residency at the Horseshoe. This annual stretch of shows that would go on long after last call Cohen dubbed the "Fall Nationals."

Another thing the pair started in their era was honouring the past by paying respect to the history and tradition of the Horseshoe by celebrating its milestone birthdays, beginning with its fiftieth in 1997. Every year of a major birthday, the bar would have a week-long bash with special programming over the course of four nights, each weekend in December (you'll recall the Horseshoe opened on December 9 back in 1947). They brought back many of the Canadian bands who had played there and made their mark back in the mid-eighties and early nineties — bands like 54-40, Spirit of

Horseshoe Tavern part-owner and booking agent Craig Laskey.

the West, the Watchmen, and Blue Rodeo. They also started documenting the new era, decorating the walls across from the bar in the front room with set lists, framed photographs, and newspaper clippings of all the bands that have played there during their tenure. Cohen gives credit to his wife for that idea. "We respect the past, but it's also about making our own thing go. We've mainly collected memorabilia from our era. There are pictures on the walls of Great Big Sea, the Old 97's, the Jayhawks, and Spirit of the West, all bands who played here from 1994 on.

"If you are stuck in doing it the same ways it was done before, it's going to fail," says Cohen. "No offence to the hipster kids. You have to modernize, but it's sometimes a fine line. We've tweaked the Horseshoe logo over the years, and we now have cash registers that go to a central computer system."

After three years, Jeff was getting antsy and told Craig they needed to do something different. He told him that he was done working for other people, and then he told Sprackman as well:

> If I'm going to do this for a living, I want to own my own
> club. I need to be an owner, so I told Kenny that we were

thinking of leaving. He asked, "What are you going to do?" I said, "The El Mo is sitting there empty. I think we are going to go buy the building and do what we've been doing here."

Kenny just looked at me and said, "I don't want to compete with you. Do you want to become a partner?" He had no interest in buying another club, so he said, "Why don't you just buy into the Horseshoe?" [This was February 1998. Cohen was dumbstruck.]

"Is it for sale?" I asked. He said X-Ray was thinking of getting out of the business, to go talk to him, so I went to Austin where X-Ray was spending some time.

He told me he was thinking of getting out: "Can you pay me a decent amount?"

"Of course," I said, and we reached a deal.

He took a lump-sum payment, and I bought him out. On August 1, 1998, I became an owner of the Horseshoe Tavern. Part of my deal as an owner was to invest fifty thousand dollars into the business.

Horseshoe Tavern majority owner Jeff Cohen.

As part of that capital investment, Cohen put in the first draft taps the Horseshoe had ever had in the front bar.

As owner, Jeff elevated Craig to chief talent buyer. One of the other changes that have been made in the Cohen and Laskey era was increasing the legal capacity from 167 (even though they were cramming 400 people in most weekends) to 468. They kept getting fined by the police or the Alcohol and Gaming Commission, and it wasn't worth the hassle anymore; it also didn't make good business sense. Cohen also ended up having to put one hundred thousand dollars into the club to change the HVAC system and upgrade the washrooms. "I modernized the place without taking away its physical beauty," says Cohen. "We also added new sound systems for the stage, new carpet, but made sure the black-and-white checkerboard tile on the floor made famous by The Hip song remained. We also hired a guy who restored all the wood in the place to make it look traditional. We modernized the banking and credit card point-of-sale payment systems and made ticketing deals with Ticketmaster and Ticketfly. We also set up standardized, more professional relationships with our staff, hired bar managers and a professional accountant. We basically changed the business structure."

Jesse Malin gets down on his knees and personal with the crowd, singing on the checkerboard floor at the Horseshoe Tavern on January 22, 2011.

Colin James returned to the Horseshoe Tavern for the first time in twenty years in the fall of 2016 to play a short gig, launching his latest album, *Blue Highways*.

"Everyone will talk about the music and the bands who played here, but the fact of the matter is a bar does not stay open this long without an owner, whether it's Kenny, X-Ray, me, the Clairmans, or the original owner, Jack Starr, that has savvy business skills that can make it work in every era," Cohen explains.

While Cohen bought 50 percent of the business from X-Ray, all the while he learned the ins and outs of the business from Sprackman. Eventually, he started renegotiating the leases with the Clairmans and took over the day-to-day running of the business to the point that Kenny decided to retire in 2005. Sprackman is still a silent partner and owns 15 percent of the business. When he retired, he took 35 percent from his 50 percent and sold 25 percent of it to Craig and 10 percent to the 'Shoe's in-house accountant Naomi Montpetit. Ever since, the three of them have owned and operated the club. To keep it going, along the line, they've expanded their little music empire — from creating a promotion company called Collective Concerts, to buying Lee's Palace, to more recently running the three-day outdoor Toronto Urban Roots Festival (TURF) each September. "It sounds crazy, but we have the same booking policy we had when we came in back in 1995," says Cohen.

Conclusion

The Next Seventy Years
Are Anyone's Guess

AS YOU FINISH FLIPPING THROUGH these pages, the inevitable question that comes to mind is this: What's next for the grande dame that has stood tall at Queen and Spadina for seventy years? With a lease signed by Cohen and crew for a couple more years, the short term is in good hands. After that, it's anyone's guess. One thing is sure: it would be a sad day, not only for Toronto but also for Canada, if the legendary Horseshoe Tavern was no more. Here's hoping that no matter what happens — even if Cohen decides to retire down the road — the Clairman family will decide not to sell out to the highest bidder and to keep the house that Jack built alive, to offer many more generations of musicians a place to play and music lovers a shrine to come worship their favourite bands and enjoy live music with like-minded souls.

Jeff Cohen and Craig Laskey recently celebrated their twentieth year at the helm. For a pair who started with a two-year plan, that's pretty impressive. "We haven't gone bankrupt or fired ourselves," Cohen jokes. "I might start to look eventually for somebody to bring in to hand the business over to, but until then we are ready to celebrate our seventieth birthday." (These anniversary shows and parties were in the works as this book went to print.)

When Cohen is asked what's next, he thinks for a minute, then replies, "Hopefully we will keep it going as long as we can. We have a lease on the building signed with the Clairmans until 2018, and all indications show they will renew this again for another five or ten years."

Owners and operators at the Horseshoe, before and after Cohen, have tried to keep this place at Queen and Spadina through rising rents. A few failed. Most succeeded. You never know whether the landlord might turn around one day and decide it's time to cash in. The Clairman family now owns 100 percent of the building — they recently bought out the other 50 percent stake owned by one of Jack Starr's sons.

In the meantime, Cohen, Laskey, and the rest of the 'Shoe's team will carry the weight of the tavern's legacy and try to keep the place running. The current majority owner says that it's not that easy. There's a lot more to running a bar today than there was back in Starr's day. The biggest hurdle and challenge is navigating changing municipal bylaws and reams of red tape. Cohen admits he's always worried that the rise in litigation in the States over slips and falls in public spaces might start to be seen in Canada as well. Sure, they have liability insurance, but one never knows. The legal costs could be crippling. "That's always in the back of [one's] head," he says.

Another big challenge is ever-increasing government regulations — from the Alcohol and Gaming Commission of Ontario to the province and local government. "It's become a bureaucratic nightmare," Cohen explains. "There are so many rules. Any night you go to any bar, a rule is being broken somewhere. It's getting harder to do business with so many regulations that were written by people who have never owned, or most likely been in, a bar or even involved in the alcohol business."

Cohen has stories that could fill pages. Every few years, government inspectors show up and try to tell him he is in violation of some bylaw or another. Once, a couple of years back, the City of Toronto municipal licensing folks claimed his patio was not of the same design that was stamped and approved back in 1982. He asked to see the drawing. On inspection, he told them, "I can't have that design anymore because the fire inspector won't allow a railing to go through the front door!"

He's grown good at playing the political game and dealing with all these distractions, but it's just one more hassle and reality of running the Horseshoe Tavern in 2017. "The City of Toronto is trying to regulate us to death," he says.

Now in his mid-fifties, Cohen sees himself as a mentor and industry leader and veteran who needs to take a stand against these growing issues to help out his peers. He's starting to get involved with local politics, and recently helped start an organization called Music Canada Live to be the voice of Canada's live music industry, advancing and promoting its many economic, social, and cultural benefits. He advocates on its behalf to the government and to the media on issues impacting the live music industry.

At some point, Cohen may just decide he wants to get out of the business even though he loves it to death. When that time comes, he may be looking for the right person to take over, just as he and Craig were the right ones to carry on the Kenny and X-Ray era. That's a question best left to another day. As Cohen says, "It's been around for seventy years. Where do you think it's going? It's still a barometer of what a band is worth at a certain level in Canada."

There definitely needs to be a succession plan, but until then, I encourage you to do your part to support live music wherever you live. At the end of the day, that's what will keep clubs like the Horseshoe Tavern open and viable for the next generation. I hope this book has inspired you to go see a band play tonight — maybe, if you live in or near Toronto, at the 'Shoe. What are you waiting for? The walls at 370 Queen Street West are whispering your name.

Acknowledgements

A project of this magnitude is never possible without the support and guidance of many. First, I must thank fellow scribe John Goddard, who tipped me off to the fact that Dundurn Press was interested in music-related book titles. Due to a chance meeting and conversation with Goddard at another of my favourite music bars (the Dakota Tavern), the seeds for this project were born.

Much appreciation goes out to all of the musicians, fellow journalists, past owners, and music industry insiders who took time away from their busy schedules to reminisce and share with me some stories about their Horseshoe days. A special shout-out to current majority owners Jeff Cohen and Craig Laskey, who supported the project from the start; they helped me locate — and connected me with — sources and shared key contacts and photos for this book, without which this project would have been incomplete. I would be remiss if I didn't also thank Blue Rodeo's Jim Cuddy for contributing the foreword to this book and his management, Starfish Entertainment, for providing easy access to the artists they represent and for contributing key photos. Thanks also to the Clairman family (Gary and his mother, Natalie), who helped fill gaps in the bar's early history, recalling tales of their father and grandfather — original owner Jack Starr — as well as providing images.

Thanks to everyone at Dundurn Press for believing in this book and getting excited about this project from the first day I pitched the idea. Special thanks go to president and publisher Kirk Howard, who took a chance on a first-time author; my editor Allison Hirst, who took my words, provided constructive feedback throughout the past eighteen months, and helped to massage those words into the finished manuscript. Thanks are also due to the sales and marketing team: Jaclyn Hodsdon, Beth Bruder, Margaret Bryant, Synora Van Drine, Kate Condon-Moriarty, Michelle Melski, Kendra Martin, Jen Mannering, Kyle Gray, Andre Bovee-Begun, and Sheila Douglas.

Thank you also to my high school creative writing teacher, Barb Carter. For without her writing class and her encouragement, I might never have fully developed my talent and believed that writing as a career was possible. Her words that she always shared with our class still ring in my ears: "Here's your assignment, should you choose to accept it — and you will!" I'm glad I always heeded that advice, as it's opened up many writing opportunities over the past couple of decades. Here's to never turning down another assignment.

To my parents, for always believing in me and for allowing me to follow my writing dreams. When I left a high-paying corporate job five years ago to pursue freelance writing full-time, they were surprised, but their support never wavered. My dad (an academic and a published author) was always my best editor growing up. He helped me hone my writing skills. From him, I learned to simplify my sentences and cut the clutter. Before submitting this manuscript, he proofed many of the chapters. Thanks, Dad.

Finally, thanks to my family: to my wonderful children, Alex and Isabella, for leaving Daddy alone when he was working extra hours in the basement office, and to my wife, Patricia, who deserves a parade for all she's done. She is my best editor. She is my lifelong friend. She's my constant companion and my cheerleader any time I feel I can't write another word. I'm so lucky to have her there on this journey, encouraging me to just put my pen to the paper or my fingers to the keyboard on those days when I feel overwhelmed or too tired, or doubt my ability. *Gracias, Corazón.*

∗   ∗   ∗

Acknowledgement is hereby made for permission to quote song material from the following publishers and copyright holders, to whom all rights are reserved.

"Bright Lights And Country Music." Written by Bill Anderson and Jimmy Gately. Copyright © 1963. Published by Johnny Bienstock Music LLC. Lyrics reprinted with permission of the publisher.

"Horseshoe Hotel Song." Written by Stompin' Tom Connors. Copyright © 1971. Lyrics reprinted with permission of the Connors family.

"Outskirts." Written by Greg Keelor and Jim Cuddy. Copyright © 1987. Published by Thunderhawk Music. Lyrics reprinted with permission of the publisher.

"Crazy Days." Written by Joey Serlin. Copyright © 1992. Published by Permusic. Lyrics reprinted with permission of the publisher.

Sources

A NOTE ABOUT SOURCES

As I researched and wrote *The Legendary Horseshoe Tavern*, I relied mostly on first-person interviews with artists, musicians, promoters, and current and past owners and bookers. I also relied heavily on the archives of the *Toronto Star* and the *Globe and Mail*.

INTERVIEWS

Adams, Chef (Adam Edward Semeniuk)
Anderson, Bill
Anderson, Cleave
Andrews, Mickey
Berg, Moe
Bidini, Dave
Bookman, Dave "Bookie"
Borra, John
Brown, Doreen
Brunton, Colin
Burke, Johnny
Caton, John
Cash, Andrew
Clairman, Gary
Clairman, Natalie
Cohen, Jeff

Cormier, Gary
Cuddy, Jim
Cummins, Patrick
Dean, Sean
deCarle, Russell
Donovan, Bazil
Doucet, Luke
Duperron, Lin
Finkelstein, Bernie
Finlayson, Josh
Fisher, Alan
Flohil, Richard
Fury, Teddy
Gardiner, Bob
Gavin, John
Goddard, John

Goddard, Peter
Gold, Jake
Greaves, Danny
Hawkins, Ron
Ingram, Jack
James, Ralph
Keelor, Greg
Koch, Steve
Langford, Jon
Laskey, Craig
Lawrence, Grant
LeDrew, Gary
Linden, Colin
MacRae, X-Ray
Martin, Jennifer

Matsell, Yvonne
Maynard, Bob
McLean, Steve
Penney, Roy
Rusk, Harry
Serlin, Joey
Sprackman, Kenny
Stanley, Steve
Topp, Gary
Tucker, Wayne
Wall, Michael T.
Waters, Sneezy
Whiteley, Ken
Wilson, Tom

WORKS

Across This Land with Stompin' Tom Connors, DVD. Directed by John C.W. Saxton. Montreal: Cinépix, 1973.

Anderson, Bill. *Still*. Decca 33 1/3 RPM, 1963. Liner notes.

Barclay, Michael. "The Try-ing Times of Blue Rodeo." *Maclean's*, November 9, 2012.

Barclay, Michael, Ian A.D. Jack, and Jason Schneider. *Have Not Been the Same: The CanRock Renaissance 1985–1995*. Toronto: ECW, 2011.

Batten, Jack. "Aunt Bea's Nashville Room." *Toronto Daily Star*, November 1, 1969.

———. "C&W Seeking a New Audience." *Globe and Mail*, February 5, 1972.

———. "George Hamilton IV: Country Sound Although His Suit's Not Nashville!" *Globe and Mail*, March 20, 1971.

"Being Hank Is Nothin' to Sneeze At." *Toronto Star*, December 2, 1978.

Benson, Denise. *Then and Now: Toronto Nightlife History: The Stories of 48 Influential Clubs from 1975–2015*. Toronto: Three O'Clock Press, 2015.

Berg, Moe. "For the Love of Music." *Toronto Star*, December 2, 2007.

"Board Stern to Dilatory Liquor License Seekers; Pastors Denounce Bars." *Globe and Mail*, March 19, 1947.

Bradburn, Jamie. "Mapping Our Music: The 1980s." *Torontoist*, August 21, 2012. http://torontoist.com/2012/08/mapping-our-music-the-1980s.

Brewster, Ariel. "When a New Wave Washed Over Stuffy Old Toronto." *Globe and Mail*, May 31, 2008.

Brown, Dick. "The Horseshoe Tavern Had Faith." *Globe and Mail*, April 14, 1973.

Burliuk, Greg. "Blue Rodeo Band Offers Familiar Charms with Blue Tunes to 'Make the Sad Happy.'" *Whig-Standard*, December 6, 1985.

Cameron House Records. "Handsome Ned." http://www.cameronhouse records.com/gallery/handsome-ned.

Champion, Luke. "Get to Know a Bartender: Teddy Fury of The Horseshoe Tavern." *BlogTO*, March 22, 2012. http://www.blogto.com/people/2012/03/get_to_know_a_bartender_teddy_fury_of_the_horseshoe_tavern.

Clark, Mandy. "The Shoe: 65 Years of Horseshoe Tavern History." *Global News* video, 14:26. Produced by Mia Sheldon. January 23, 2013. http://globalnews.ca/video/398352/the-shoe-65-years-of-horseshoe-tavern-history.

Cole, Susan G. "The 'Shoe Staggers but Keeps Rolling." *NOW Magazine*, December 6, 2007.

Connors, Tom. *Stompin' Tom: Before the Fame*. Toronto: Viking, 1995.

———. *Stompin' Tom and the Connors Tone*. Toronto: Viking, 2000.

Crawford, Blair. "Maynard Collins (1946–2015) — Playwright Wrote *Hank Williams: The Show He Never Gave*." *Ottawa Citizen*, November 27, 2015.

Dafoe, Chris. "Storied Bar Bellies Up to Its 40th Year." *Globe and Mail*, December 9, 1987.

Davey, Steven. "Bygone Beverley." *NOW Magazine*, December 18, 2003.

"The Dick Nolan Story." *The Performance Hour*. CBC Radio, May 15, 2004.

DiManno, Rosie. "Bottom Line Guy." *Toronto Star*, March 25, 1988.

———. "Ex-Cop Kruk is X-L Boys' Idea Man." *Toronto Star*, March 24, 1988.

———. "The XL Boys." *Toronto Star*, March 25, 1988.

———. "X-Ray Is Team's Gentle Giant." *Toronto Star*, March 24, 1988.

Duff, Morris. "Make Way for the Country Sound." *Toronto Daily Star*, March 21, 1964.

Edwardson, Ryan. *Canuck Rock: A History of Canadian Popular Music*. Toronto: University of Toronto Press, 2009.

Escott, Colin. *I Saw the Light: The Story of Hank Williams.* New York: Back Bay Books, 2004.

Finkelstein, Bernie. *True North: A Life in the Music Business.* Toronto: McClelland & Stewart, 2012.

Fisher, Alan. *God, Sex and Rock 'n' Roll: One Man's Spiritual Awakening.* Bloomington, IN: Xlibris Corporation, 2011.

Fruitman, Steve. *Stevedore Steve* (blog). http://www.backtothesugar camp.com/stevedore.htm.

Gavin, John. "Exclusive Interview with Roy Payne." *Atlantic Seabreeze.*

"George Hamilton IV — Obituary." *Telegraph,* September 18, 2014. http://www.telegraph.co.uk/news/obituaries/11105769/George-Hamilton-IV-obituary.html.

Gilday, Katherine. "New Wave Duo Heading for the Last Bound-Up." *Globe and Mail*, December 2, 1978.

Goddard, John, and Richard Crouse. *Rock and Roll Toronto: From Alanis to Zeppelin.* Toronto: Doubleday, 1997.

Goddard, Peter. "Country Music's Horseshoe Club Changing Image." *Toronto Star.*

———. "That Good Old Country Music Sweeping the Country." *Toronto Star,* April 21, 1973.

———. "The Reggae Beat Grabs the Kids from the Suburbs." *Toronto Star*, April 29, 1978.

———. "The Shoe Still Fits After All These Years." *Toronto Star.* January 31, 1998. M14.

Gray, Jeff. "The Fight of the Matador: A New Owner Struggles to Revive the Legendary Toronto Booze Can." *Globe and Mail,* May 13, 2016.

Hamilton IV, George. *Canadian Pacific. 33 1/3 RPM* RCAVictor, 1969. Liner notes.

Heydorn, Bernard. "Finding the Heart of Canada." *Toronto Star*, May 7, 2002.

Holland, Doug. "The Horseshoe Tavern Club Gig." *It's Only Rock 'n' Roll*, Rolling Stones Fan Club of Europe magazine, October 2007.

Hollett, Michael. "Handsome Ned: The Second Coming of the King of Queen." *NOW Magazine*, January 10, 2008.

Howell, Peter. "The Hip Hit the Horseshoe to Introduce New Songs." *Toronto Star*, April 20, 1992.

Hutchinson, Thomas, comp. *Hutchinson's Toronto Directory, 1862–1863.* Toronto: Lovell & Gibson, 1862.

Jennings, Nicholas. *Before the Gold Rush.* Toronto: Viking, 1997.

Jones, Alan. "Revisiting Toronto's Forgotten Punk Scene." *Vice*, February 26, 2014. http://noisey.vice.com/en_ca/article/revisiting-torontos-forgotten-70s-punk-scene.

Kirby, Blaik. "A Hurtin' Blue Collar TV's Link to Common Man." *The Globe and Mail*, June 1, 1974.

Kirkland, Bruce. "New Horseshoe Certainly Has Its Surprises."

Kosser, Michael. *How Nashville Became Music City, U.S.A.: 50 Years of Music Row.* Milwaukee: Hal Leonard, 2006.

Kustanczy, Catherine. "Looking Back at Toronto's Radical 1980s Underground Art Scene." *Hyperallergic*, March 28, 2016. http://hyperallergic.com/285738/looking-back-at-torontos-radical-1980s-underground-art-scene.

Lacey, Liam. "A Country Music Era Ends with the Horseshoe's Death." *Globe and Mail*, December 4, 1982.

———. "Good News, Music From Queen Street." *Globe and Mail*, February 14, 1984.

———. "Ned Takes Country Downtown." *Globe and Mail*, February 14, 1985.

Lamb, Marjorie and Barry Pearson. *The Boyd Gang.* Toronto: Peter Martin and Associates, 1976.

The Last Pogo, DVD. Directed by Colin Brunton. Toronto: Dream Tower Records, 2008.

The Last Pogo Jumps Again: Punk's Last Waltz, DVD. Directed by Colin Brunton. Toronto: Ontario Limited, 2013.

Leckie, Steven. "550 Kids: The Real Show at Punk Rock's Last Stand." *Toronto Star*, December 2, 1978.

MacInnis, Craig. "A Toronto Band on the Outskirts of the Big Time." *Toronto Star*, December 18, 1988.

Malone, Bill C. Malone. *Country Music, U.S.A.,* 2nd ed. Austin: University of Texas Press, 1985.

Marcus, Greil. *Mystery Train: Images of America in Rock 'n' Roll Music.* New York: Plume, 2015.

Marquis, Greg. "Confederation's Casualties: 'The Maritimer' as a Problem in 1960s Toronto," *Acadiensis* 39, no. 1 (Winter/Spring 2010): 83–107.

Meeker, Geoff. "The Incredible Saga of Roy Payne." *Newfoundland Herald,* January 3, 1987.

Mersereau, Bob. *The History of Canadian Rock 'n' Roll.* Milwaukee: Backbeat Books, 2015.

Moore, Thurston. *The Country Music Who's Who.* Heather Publications, 1965.

Neister, Alan. "Dick Dale Influential Guitarist Was Worth the Wait." *Globe and Mail,* October 5, 1995.

———. "Music Review: Vic Chesnutt." *Globe and Mail,* March 20, 1997.

O'Malley, Martin. "Roy Payne: A Bitter Boy from Newfoundland Is Getting Some Breaks in a Town He Hates." *Globe and Mail.*

Perlich, Tim. "From Cool Country to Punk Rock Chaos," *NOW magazine,* December 6, 2007. http://nowtoronto.com/music/from-cool-country-to-punk-rock-chaos.

———. "Long Thought Lost Handsome Ned Recordings Being Released," *The Perlich Post* (blog), January 14, 2017. http://theperlichpost.blogspot.ca/2017/01/long-thought-lost-handsome-ned.html.

Pevere, Geoff. *Gods of the Hammer: The Teenage Head Story.* Toronto: Coach House, 2014.

Potter, Mitch. "And the Band Played On …" *Toronto Star,* March 13, 1989.

Powell, Betsey. "Stones Roll In, Tavern Rocks During Surprise Gig on Queen. Mick Jagger Thanks Toronto for Hospitality." *Toronto Star,* September 5, 2007.

Quill, Greg. "Honky-Tonking Heart and Soul." *Toronto Star,* February 14, 1986.

Scallan, Niamh. "If These Walls Could Talk." *Toronto Star,* October 30, 2011.

Schmatta: Rags to Riches to Rags. Directed by Marc Levin. 2009.

"Sneezy Waters' Other Life as Hank Williams." *Toronto Star,* December 2, 1978.

"Stompin' Tom: Once a Drifter Playing for Dimes, He Sings About Canadian Cities With Love." *Globe and Mail.* Previously published in *The Last Post,* by Mark Starowicz.

Streissguth, Michael. *Outlaw: Waylon, Willie, Kris, and the Renegades of Nashville.* New York: It Books, 2013.

Sutherland, Sam. *Perfect Youth: The Birth of Canadian Punk.* Toronto: ECW, 2012.

Toronto Directory 1929. Metropolitan Toronto Library Canadian History 8 (1929): 1657.

Toronto Directory 1940. Metropolitan Toronto Library Canadian History 9 (1940): 391.

Toushek, Gary. "Luck of the Horseshoe." *Globe and Mail*, March 8, 1978.

Vallée, Brian. *Edwin Alonzo Boyd: The Story of the Notorious Boyd Gang*. Toronto: Doubleday, 1997.

Wickens, Barbara. "Some Stones Fans Get Lucky." *Maclean's*, September 22, 1997.

Wiseman, Mac. *At the Toronto Horseshoe Club*. CD, 1965, Wise. Liner notes.

Wolff, Kurt. *Country Music: The Rough Guide*. London: Rough Guides, 2000.

Worth, Liz. "A Picture and a Thousand Words: Liz Worth on Toronto's Original Punk Scene, and How It Changed a City." *Toronto Star*, November 26, 2006.

———. *Treat Me Like Dirt: An Oral History of Punk in Toronto and Beyond 1977–1981*. Toronto: Bongo Beat/ECW, 2009.

W.R. Brown. *Brown's Toronto General Directory 1861*. Toronto: W.C. Chewett & Co., 1861.

WEBSITES

Blue Rodeo's official site — www.bluerodeo.com

Canadian Music Hall of Fame — www.canadianmusichalloffame.ca

Gary's Bar — garysbar.blogspot.ca

Hank Williams's official site — www.hankwilliams.com

The Last Pogo Jumps Again — www.thelastpogo.net

The Legendary Horseshoe Tavern — www.horseshoetavern.com

Punks and Rockers — punksandrockers.com/toronto-punk-history-2/

Image Credits

15: Steffen Paulus
19: The Ontario Jewish Archives
21: Courtesy of the Clairman Family
22: Courtesy of the Clairman Family
23: City of Toronto Archives
24 (top and bottom): City of Toronto Archives
29: Courtesy of Michael T. Wall
33: Courtesy of Roy Penney
36: Courtesy of the Clairman Family
39: Courtesy of the Clairman Family
40: City of Toronto Archives/ Morgan Ross
43: Courtesy of Bill Anderson
44: Courtesy of Roy Penney
45: Courtesy of the Clairman Family
50: Courtesy of the Clairman Family
51: Courtesy of Wayne Tucker
53: Courtesy of Greg Dunning
62: Courtesy of Greg Dunning

64: Courtesy of Ed Preston
66: Courtesy of Michael T. Wall
67 (top and bottom): Courtesy of Ed Preston
70: Courtesy of Ken Whiteley
74: Courtesy of Gary Topp
77: Courtesy of Colin Brunton
80: Patrick Cummins
82: Patrick Cummins
85 (top): Courtesy of Gary Topp
85 (bottom): Courtesy of Lin Duperron
88: Patrick Cummins
90: Patrick Cummins
91: Edie Steiner
95: Courtesy of Peter W. Lamb
97: Courtesy of Peter W. Lamb
114: Patrick Cummins
123: Courtesy of Blue Rodeo/ Starfish Entertainment
124: Courtesy of Ross Taylor
129: Courtesy of the Clairman Family
130: Courtesy of X-Ray MacRae

132: Courtesy of United Talent Agency

134: Steffen Paulus

140 (all): Beth Hamill

144 (top and bottom): Courtesy of Colin Linden

157: Tom Sandler

158: Richard Beland

161: Jennifer Rowsom

171: Courtesy of Grant Lawrence

173: Beth Hamill

175: Steffen Paulus

177: Steffen Paulus

178: Steffen Paulus

180: Dundurn Press

181: Dundurn Press

182: Steffen Paulus

183: Dawn Hamilton

Index

About the Author

Ever since attending his first rock concert in 1989 (The Who) and buying his first LP (*Freeze Frame* by the J. Geils Band), music has been the elixir of David's life. With more than eighteen thousand songs on his iPod and an ever-growing vintage vinyl collection, it's a joy for him to discover new music. He loves sharing these discoveries with his wife and two children. David watched his first show at the Horseshoe Tavern, the Old 97's, more than twenty years ago; immediately, he was hooked. A regular contributor to *Words & Music, Hamilton Magazine,* and *No Depression,* over the years his writing on music has also appeared in *Paste, American Songwriter, Bluegrass Unlimited, Exclaim!* and *Canadian Musician.* As president and chief creative officer of McPherson Communications, David helps clients get their words right. He lives in Waterloo, Ontario.

horseshoetavernbook.com
www.facebook.com/horseshoetavernbook
twitter.com/mcphersoncomm
www.instagram.com/mcphersoncomm

dundurn.com   dundurnpress
@dundurnpress   dundurnpress
dundurnpress   info@dundurn.com

FIND US ON NETGALLEY & GOODREADS TOO!

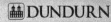
DUNDURN